Service-Oriented Architecture: An Integration Blueprint

A real-world SOA strategy for the integration of heterogeneous Enterprise systems

Successfully implement your own enterprise integration architecture using the Trivadis Integration Architecture Blueprint

Guido Schmutz

Daniel Liebhart

Peter Welkenbach

BIRMINGHAM - MUMBAI

Service-Oriented Architecture: An Integration Blueprint
A real-world SOA strategy for the integration of heterogeneous Enterprise systems

Copyright © 2010 Packt Publishing

All rights reserved. No part of this book may be reproduced, stored in a retrieval system, or transmitted in any form or by any means, without the prior written permission of the publisher, except in the case of brief quotations embedded in critical articles or reviews.

Every effort has been made in the preparation of this book to ensure the accuracy of the information presented. However, the information contained in this book is sold without warranty, either express or implied. Neither the authors, nor Packt Publishing, and its dealers and distributors will be held liable for any damages caused or alleged to be caused directly or indirectly by this book.

Packt Publishing has endeavored to provide trademark information about all of the companies and products mentioned in this book by the appropriate use of capitals. However, Packt Publishing cannot guarantee the accuracy of this information.

First published: June 2010

Production Reference: 1160610

Published by Packt Publishing Ltd.
32 Lincoln Road
Olton
Birmingham, B27 6PA, UK.

ISBN 978-1-849681-04-9

www.packtpub.com

Cover Image by Sandeep Babu (sandyjb@gmail.com)

Credits

Authors
Guido Schmutz
Daniel Liebhart
Peter Welkenbach

Reviewers
Albert Blarer
Tony Fräfel
Christoph Pletz
Patrick Blaser
Karsten Krösch

Acquisition Editor
James Lumsden

Development Editor
Stephanie Moss

Technical Editor
Ishita Dhabalia

Indexer
Rekha Nair

Editorial Team Leader
Gagandeep Singh

Project Team Leader
Lata Basantani

Project Coordinator
Sneha Harkut

Proofreader
Sandra Hopper

Graphics
Nilesh Mohite
Geetanjali Sawant
Alwin Roy

Production Coordinator
Alwin Roy

Cover Work
Alwin Roy

Foreword

Developing integration solutions is not a simple task, despite the fact that the integration of individual databases, applications, and complete systems is increasingly becoming part of software engineers' day-to-day work. In addition, developers of **Enterprise Service Buses (ESBs)**; **Enterprise Information Integration (EII)** infrastructures; messaging systems; service-oriented architecture (**SOA**) frameworks; Extract, Transform, and Load (ETL) tools; and software for data integration, all take very different approaches, and many organizations already have one or more different integration solutions in place. The Trivadis Integration Architecture Blueprint is the result of work on a large number of projects (not all of them successful), of detailed discussions with customers and specialists, and of careful study of the technical literature.

The development of the integration blueprint took several months, as the main objective was to structure the integration solution in such a way that standardized, tried-and-tested basic components could be combined to form a functioning whole, with the help of tools and other products. It was also important that the solution met customers' requirements, and could be implemented without the excessive use of resources.

We believe that by structuring the integration layer into different, clearly defined levels and layers, and by assigning best practice patterns to these layers, we can make the process of developing integration solutions significantly simpler in practice.

The concept behind the Trivadis Integration Architecture Blueprint was developed by the authors, together with Fernand Hänggi and Albert Blarer, and formulated by Daniel Liebhart, Guido Schmutz, and Peter Welkenbach. Large parts of the book have been revised several times by the authors, and have also been the subject of intense debates in workshops. We would like to thank the reviewers Albert Blarer, Patrick Blaser, Christoph Pletz, and Karsten Krösch and, in particular, Tony Fräfel for his detailed input.

Further technical information is available on our website (www.trivadis.com) in the download area and the blog (under Know-How Community).

We would like to thank everyone who has contributed to this book in any way. This includes, in particular, the reviewers and our patient colleagues who were always prepared to discuss things in detail, and clarify any number of aspects of the book. We would also like to thank our customers and business partners, with whom we have worked on a variety of projects that have given us many interesting and enriching experiences. Finally, we would like to thank our colleagues, friends, families, the proofreaders, and the publishers for their patience.

About the Authors

Guido Schmutz has worked as a software developer, IT consultant, lead architect, trainer, and coach for more than 20 years. As head of the Application Development area of the Trivadis Technology Center, he has written numerous technical publications, developed IT strategies, courses, and technocircles and spoken at international conferences. Guido Schmutz is responsible for innovating, designing, and implementing many data warehouse, customer relationship management (CRM), customer satisfaction measurement (CSM), management information system (MIS), and Enterprise Application Architecture (EAI) solutions for international banks, pharmaceutical companies, public authorities, and logistics companies. He specializes in enterprise architecture, bi-temporal data management, Java Persistence, and the Spring framework. You can contact him at `guido.schmutz@trivadis.com`.

Daniel Liebhart has more than 20 years experience of IT, and 10 years experience of managing IT services and product development. His industry and technical knowledge covers the design, architecture, implementation, and operation of complex, international systems in telecommunications, financial services, logistics, and the manufacturing industry. Daniel Liebhart is passionate about IT. He has received a number of awards and he gives lectures on software architecture and business informatics at the Hochschule für Technik in Zurich. You can reach him at `daniel.liebhart@trivadis.com`.

Peter Welkenbach works as a consultant, senior architect, and trainer in the fields of requirement engineering, object-oriented methodologies, software engineering, and quality management. He has more than 20 years experience of designing and implementing complex information systems for banks, automotive manufacturers, and pharmaceutical companies. For 10 years he has been a technology evangelist for Java technology and the use of the corresponding frameworks in customer projects. His current technical focus is model-driven software development, the Unified Modeling Language (UML), aspect-oriented programming, Java Server Faces (JSF), asynchronous Java Script, and XML (AJAX) and architecture design methodology. Peter Welkenbach is a course developer, author of numerous publications, and speaker at JAX and international Oracle conferences. He has been using Spring in numerous customer projects since it first appeared in summer 2003. You can get in touch with Welkenbach at `peter.welkenbach@trivadis.com`.

Table of Contents

Preface   1

Chapter 1: Basic Principles   7
- **Integration**   7
  - Concepts   9
    - A2A, B2B, and B2C   10
  - Integration types   11
    - Information portals   11
    - Shared data   11
    - Shared business functions   12
    - Differences between EAI and SOA   12
  - Semantic integration and the role of data   13
  - Enterprise Application Integration (EAI)   14
    - Levels of integration   16
  - Messaging   16
  - Publish/subscribe   17
  - Message brokers   18
  - Messaging infrastructure   20
  - Enterprise Service Bus   21
    - The core functions of an ESB   21
    - The structure of an ESB   22
  - Middleware   23
    - Middleware communication methods   23
    - Middleware base technologies   24
    - Routing schemes   25
- **Integration architecture variants**   26
  - Point-to-point architecture   27
  - Hub-and-spoke architecture   28
  - Pipeline architecture   29
  - Service-oriented architecture   30

Patterns for EAI/EII — 31
Direct connection — 32
Uses — 33
Broker — 33
Uses — 34
Router — 35
Uses — 36
Patterns for data integration — 37
Federation — 37
Uses — 38
Population — 38
Uses — 39
Synchronization — 40
Uses — 41
Multi-step synchronization — 41
Patterns for service-oriented integration — 42
Process integration — 42
Uses — 43
Variants — 43
Workflow integration — 44
Variants — 44
Event-driven architecture — 45
Introducing EDA — 45
Event processing — 47
Simple Event Processing (SEP) — 48
Event Stream Processing (ESP) — 48
Complex Event Processing (CEP) — 48
Grid computing/Extreme Transaction Processing (XTP) — 49
Grid computing — 49
Data grids — 51
Distribution topologies — 52
Agents — 54
Execution patterns — 54
Uses — 55
XTP (Extreme Transaction Processing) — 57
XTP and CEP — 58
Solid State Disks and grids — 59
Summary — 59

Chapter 2: Base Technologies — 61
Transactions — 63
Transactional systems — 63
Isolation levels — 66
Serializable — 66
Repeatable read — 67

Read committed	67
Read uncommitted	68
Phantom reads	68
Two-Phase Commit protocol (2PC)	69
XA transactions	70
OSGi	**72**
OSGi architecture	74
OSGi bundles	75
Collaborative model	76
Java Connector Architecture (JCA)	**76**
Uses	76
JCA components	77
Contracts	78
Java Business Integration (JBI)	**79**
JBI components	80
Service Component Architecture (SCA)	**81**
SCA specification	82
SCA elements	83
Composites	84
Service Data Objects (SDO)	**84**
SDO architecture	85
Implemented patterns	86
Process modeling	**86**
Event-driven Process Chain (EPC)	87
Business Process Modeling Notation (BPMN)	88
Business Process Execution Language (BPEL)	89
The application of process modeling	90
Summary	**90**
Chapter 3: Integration Architecture Blueprint	**91**
Dissecting the Trivadis Integration Architecture Blueprint	**91**
Standards, components, and patterns used	92
Structuring the integration blueprint	94
The road to the integration blueprint	97
Applications and integration	98
Layers in the integration solution	100
Information flow and roles	101
Information flow and building blocks	103
Combining the collection and distribution layer	104
Change of direction in the information flow	104
Adding the process layer	105
The role of the process layer	106

The building blocks of the process layer	107
Information flow in more complex integrations	108
The target becomes the source in a more complex integration	108
Routing to different target systems in the mediation layer	109
Routing to different target systems in the communication layer	110
Task sharing in the mediation layer	110
Management using a workflow building block	111
Allocating layers to levels	112
Transport level: Communication layer	**113**
Responsibility	113
Concepts and methods	114
Building blocks	114
Transport protocols	115
Transport formats	117
Integration domain level: Collection/distribution layer	**118**
Responsibility	118
Concepts and methods	118
Building blocks	119
Integration domain level: Mediation layer	**120**
Responsibility	120
Concepts and methods	120
Building blocks	121
Canonical data model	122
Message construction	124
Messaging channel	124
Message routing	125
Message transformation	126
Application level: Process layer	**126**
Responsibility	126
Concepts and methods	126
Building blocks	127
Job scheduler	127
Portal	128
Workflow	128
Event processing pattern	130
Notation and visualization	**133**
Representing the scenarios and the notation used	133
Visualizing different levels of granularity	134
Representing transaction boundaries	135
Configuration parameters as additional artifacts	136
Extension for capacity planning	136
Summary	**137**

Chapter 4: Implementation scenarios — 139
EAI/EII scenarios — 140
Implementing the direct connection business pattern — 140
Variant with synchronous call over asynchronous protocol — 141
Implementing the broker business pattern — 142
Implementing the router business pattern — 143
Service-oriented integration scenarios — 144
Implementing the process integration business pattern — 144
Variant with externalized business rules in a rule engine — 146
Variant with batch-driven integration process — 146
Implementing the workflow business pattern — 147
Data integration scenarios — 148
Implementing the federation business pattern — 148
Variant of the federation pattern using mashup technology — 149
Implementing the population business pattern — 151
Variant involving encapsulation of the population pattern as a web service — 152
Variant of the population pattern started by a change event from Change Data Capture (CDC) — 153
Variant with SOA-based population pattern triggered by a Change Data Capture event — 154
Implementing the synchronization business pattern — 155
EDA scenario — 157
Implementing the event processing business pattern — 157
Variant with two levels of complex event processing — 158
Grid computing/XTP scenario — 159
Implementing the grid computing business pattern — 160
Variant with ESB wrapping a data grid to cache service results — 160
Connecting to an SAP system — 161
Modernizing an integration solution — 162
Initial situation — 163
Sending new orders — 164
Receiving the confirmation — 165
Evaluation of the existing solution — 165
Modernizing — integration with SOA — 166
Evaluation of the new solution — 169
Trivadis Architecture Blueprints and integration — 169
Summary — 171

Chapter 5: Vendor Products for Implementing the Trivadis Blueprint — 173
Oracle Fusion Middleware product line — 173
Oracle Application Integration Architecture (AIA) — 178
Oracle Data Integrator — 180
IBM WebSphere product line — 182
IBM Information Management software — 186

Microsoft BizTalk and .NET 3.0	**188**
Microsoft SQL Server Integration Services	**192**
Spring framework combined with other open source software	**195**
Summary	**200**
Appendix: References	**201**
Index	**207**

Preface

With the widespread use of service-oriented architecture (SOA), the integration of different IT systems has gained a new relevance. The era of isolated business information systems—so-called **silos** or **stove-pipe** architectures—is finally over. It is increasingly rare to find applications developed for a specific purpose that do not need to exchange information with other systems. Furthermore, SOA is becoming more and more widely accepted as a standard architecture. Nearly all organizations and vendors are designing or implementing applications with SOA capability. SOA represents an end-to-end approach to the IT system landscape as the support function for business processes. Because of SOA, functions provided by individual systems are now available in a single standardized form throughout organizations, and even outside their corporate boundaries. In addition, SOA is finally offering mechanisms that put the focus on existing systems, and make it possible to continue to use them. Smart integration mechanisms are needed to allow existing systems, as well as the functionality provided by individual applications, to be brought together into a new fully functioning whole. For this reason, it is essential to transform the abstract concept of integration into concrete, clearly structured, and practical implementation variants.

The Trivadis Integration Architecture Blueprint indicates how integration architectures can be implemented in practice. It achieves this by representing common integration approaches, such as Enterprise Application Integration (EAI); Extract, Transform, and Load (ETL); event-driven architecture (EDA); and others, in a clearly and simply structured blueprint. It creates transparency in the confused world of product developers and theoretical concepts.

The Trivadis Integration Architecture Blueprint shows how to structure, describe, and understand existing application landscapes from the perspective of integration. The process of developing new systems is significantly simplified by dividing the integration architecture into process, mediation, collection and distribution, and communication layers. The blueprint makes it possible to implement application systems correctly without losing sight of the bigger picture: a high performance, flexible, scalable, and affordable enterprise architecture.

The background: Integration instead of isolation

Many enterprises are converting their operational structure from a functional hierarchy to a process-oriented, flexible organizational form. A characteristic feature of function-oriented organizations is a vertical division into independent functions. As a result, process chains are typically interrupted at departmental boundaries. This leads to the creation of so-called **process islands**, which often fall under different areas of responsibility and administration. If the departments in question are also geographically separated, the potential for communication problems increases. In general, the formation of these islands also has an impact on the IT landscape. In such companies, there are usually large numbers of redundant applications and data islands, and integrating them represents challenges from technical, social, and organizational perspectives.

Information transparency is normally not one of the strengths of this type of organization. Instead, the necessary knowledge about implemented process logic, and the accompanying data, is stored at a departmental level in a non-transparent and incomplete form. Redundant and inconsistent data is a common challenge/problem for these companies, and the process of integrating this data is time consuming as well as costly.

As a result, function-oriented organizations have difficulties in reacting in an appropriate, agile fashion to rapidly changing markets, customer requirements, and technologies. Process-oriented organizations, on the other hand, are considerably more flexible and, from an IT perspective, have the support of corresponding process-oriented concepts, such as SOA and EDA.

Process-oriented organizations need to be supported by process-oriented IT systems. Nowadays, the close links between operational processes and the underlying IT systems, make it necessary for the IT landscape to be closely tailored to the enterprise's technical requirements, and not to be regarded simply as an end in itself. In recent years, the term "Service-Oriented Architecture" has been widely used to describe a concept that puts process-oriented, technical services at the heart of the technical perspective, with the aim of offering reusable service components which allow for the implementation of business processes in a quick, cost-effective, and easily traceable way.

If the IT landscape of a process-oriented organization is considered as a whole, strategic aspects such as the implementation of an enterprise architecture (Bernus et al. 2003), a business motivation model (Hall et al. 2005), the Open Group Architecture Framework (Haren 2007), the Zachman Framework (Zachman 2007), or process architectures, come into play. Although this approach has a very small role in the concrete implementation of applications, there is, nevertheless, a common denominator here: the integration architecture. Putting an integrated solution (based on a blueprint) in place supports the systematic and strategic implementation of an enterprise architecture.

What this book covers

Despite the wide variety of useful and comprehensive books and other publications on the subject of integration, the approaches that they describe often lack practical relevance. The basic issue involves, on the one hand, deciding how to divide an integration solution into individual areas so that it meets the customer requirements, and on the other hand, how it can be implemented with a reasonable amount of effort. In this case, this means structuring it in such a way that standardized, tried-and-tested basic components can be combined to form a functioning whole, with the help of tools and products. For this reason, the Trivadis Integration Architecture Blueprint subdivides the integration layer into further layers. This kind of layering is not common in technical literature, but it has been proven to be very useful in practice. It allows any type of integration problem to be represented, including traditional ETL (Extract, Transform, and Load), classic EAI (Enterprise Application Integration), EDA (event-driven architecture), and grid computing. This idea is reflected in the structure of the book.

Chapter 1, Basic Principles, covers the fundamental integration concepts. This chapter is intended as an introduction for specialists who have not yet dealt with the subject of integration.

Chapter 2, Base Technologies, describes a selection of base technologies. By far the most important of these are transaction strategies and their implementation, as well as process modeling. In addition, Java EE Connector Architecture (JCA), Java Business Integration (JBI), Service Component Architecture (SCA), and Service Data Objects (SDO) are explained. Many other base technologies are used in real-life integration projects, but these go beyond the scope of this book.

Chapter 3, Integration Architecture Blueprint, describes the Trivadis Integration Architecture Blueprint. The process of layering integration solutions is fully substantiated, and each step is explained on the basis of the division of work between the individual layers. After this, each of the layers and their components are described.

Chapter 4, Implementation Scenarios, demonstrates how the Trivadis Integration Architecture Blueprint represents the fundamental integration concepts that have been described in Chapter 1. We will use the blueprint with its notation and visualization to understand some common integration scenarios in a mostly product-neutral form. We will cover traditional, as well as modern, SOA-driven integration solutions.

Chapter 5, Vendor Products for Implementing the Trivadis Blueprint, completes the book with a mapping of some vendor platforms to the Trivadis Integration Architecture Blueprint.

Appendix, References holds a list of all the referenced books and articles. It's a collection of additional important and interesting material covering modern SOA-driven as well as traditional integration solution.

What you need for this book

The book assumes a comprehensive understanding of SOA; however, previous knowledge of the Trivadis Blueprint is not necessary. Those less experienced in integration will benefit from the explanation of integration concepts and terminology, while the more advanced can move straight onto getting to grips with the Blueprint's structure.

Who this book is for

This book is intended for IT professionals, architects, managers, and project managers who are responsible for planning, designing, providing, and operating integration solutions.

Conventions

In this book, you will find a number of styles of text that distinguish between different kinds of information. Here are some examples of these styles, and an explanation of their meaning.

New terms and **important words** are shown in bold.

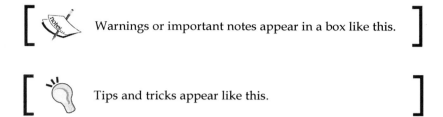

Reader feedback

Feedback from our readers is always welcome. Let us know what you think about this book—what you liked or may have disliked. Reader feedback is important for us to develop titles that you really get the most out of.

To send us general feedback, simply send an e-mail to feedback@packtpub.com, and mention the book title via the subject of your message.

If there is a book that you need and would like to see us publish, please send us a note in the **SUGGEST A TITLE** form on www.packtpub.com or e-mail suggest@packtpub.com.

Customer support

Now that you are the proud owner of a Packt book, we have a number of things to help you to get the most from your purchase.

Errata

Although we have taken every care to ensure the accuracy of our content, mistakes do happen. If you find a mistake in one of our books—maybe a mistake in the text or the code—we would be grateful if you would report this to us. By doing so, you can save other readers from frustration, and help us to improve subsequent versions of this book. If you find any errata, please report them by visiting http://www.packtpub.com/support, selecting your book, clicking on the **let us know** link, and entering the details of your errata. Once your errata are verified, your submission will be accepted and the errata added to any list of existing errata. Any existing errata can be viewed by selecting your title from http://www.packtpub.com/support.

Piracy

Piracy of copyright material on the Internet is an ongoing problem across all media. At Packt, we take the protection of our copyright and licenses very seriously. If you come across any illegal copies of our works, in any form, on the Internet, please provide us with the location address or web site name immediately so that we can pursue a remedy.

Please contact us at `copyright@packtpub.com` with a link to the suspected pirated material.

We appreciate your help in protecting our authors, and our ability to bring you valuable content.

Questions

You can contact us at `questions@packtpub.com` if you are having a problem with any aspect of the book, and we will do our best to address it.

Basic Principles

This chapter describes the fundamental concepts of integration, and is intended as an introduction to integration technology and terminology. You will:

- Learn the basic concepts, which are often used in the context of integration architecture
- Grasp an overview of the different architecture variants, such as point-to-point, hub-and-spoke, pipeline, and **service-oriented architecture (SOA)**
- Learn about service-oriented integration with an explanation of both the process and the workflow integration patterns
- Understand the different types of data integration and the accompanying patterns
- Gain an understanding of **Enterprise Application Integration (EAI)** and **Enterprise Information Integration (EII)**, and an indication of how direct connection, broker, and router patterns should be used
- Understand developments in SOA resulting from the introduction of enterprise-wide events
- Understand the integration technologies of the future: grid computing and **extreme transaction processing (XTP)**

Integration

The term *integration* has a number of different meanings. A fundamental knowledge of the terms and concepts of integration is an essential part of an integration architect's toolkit. There are many ways of classifying the different types of integration. From an enterprise-wide perspective, a distinction is made between **application-to-application (A2A)**, **business-to-business (B2B)**, and **business-to-consumer (B2C)** integration. Portal, function, and data integration can be classified on the basis of tiers. Another possible grouping consists of integration based on semantics.

Fundamental integration concepts include **Enterprise Application Integration (EAI)**, **Enterprise Service Bus (ESB)**, middleware, and messaging. These were used to define the subject before the introduction of SOA, and still form the basis of many integration projects today. EAI is, in fact, a synonym of integration. In David Linthicum's original definition of EAI, it means *the unrestricted sharing of data and business processes among any connected applications*. The technological implementation of EAI systems is, in most cases, based on middleware. The main base technology of EAI is messaging, giving the option of implementing an integration architecture through asynchronous communication, using messages which are exchanged across a distributed infrastructure and a central message broker.

The fundamental integration architecture variants are:

- point-to-point
- hub-and-spoke
- pipeline
- service-oriented architecture

A point-to-point architecture is a collection of independent systems, which are connected through a network.

Hub-and-spoke architecture represents a further stage in the evolution of application and system integration, in which a central hub takes over responsibility for communications.

In pipeline architecture, independent systems along the value-added chain are integrated using a message bus. The bus capability is the result of interfaces to the central bus being installed in a distributed manner through the communication network, which gives applications local access to a bus interface. Different applications are integrated to form a functioning whole by means of distributed and independent service calls that are orchestrated through an ESB and, if necessary, a process engine.

A fundamental technique for integration is the usage of **design patterns**. These include process and workflow patterns in a service-oriented integration, federation, population, and synchronization of patterns in a data integration, and direct connection, broker, and router patterns, which form part of EAI and EII. It is important to be familiar with all of these patterns, in order to be able to use them correctly.

The most recent integration architectures are based on concepts such as event-driven architecture, grid computing, or **extreme transaction processing (XTP)**. These technologies have yet to be tested in practice, but they are highly promising and of great interest for a number of applications, in particular, for corporate companies and large organizations.

Concepts

The Trivadis Integration Architecture Blueprint applies a clear and simple naming to each of the individual layers. However, in the context of integration, a wide range of different definitions and terms are used, which we will explain in this chapter.

- **Application to Application (A2A)**: A2A refers to the integration of applications and systems with each another.
- **Business to Business (B2B)**: B2B means the external integration of business partners', customers', and suppliers' processes and applications.
- **Business to Consumer (B2C)**: B2C describes the direct integration of end customers into internal corporate processes, for example, by means of Internet technologies.
- **Integration types**: Integration projects are generally broken down into integration portals, shared data integration, and shared function integration. Portals integrate applications at a user interface level. Shared data integration involves implementing integration architectures at a data level, and shared function integration at a function level.
- **Semantic integration**: One example of a semantic integration approach is the use of model-based semantic repositories for integrating data, using different types of contextual information.
- **Enterprise Application Integration (EAI)**: EAI allows for the unrestricted sharing of data and business processes among any connected applications.
- **Messaging, publish/subscribe, message brokers, and messaging infrastructures**: These are integration mechanisms involving asynchronous communication using messages, which are exchanged across a distributed infrastructure and a central message broker.
- **Enterprise Service Bus (ESB)**: An ESB is an integration infrastructure used to implement an EAI. The role of the ESB is to decouple client applications from services.
- **Middleware**: The technological implementation of EAI systems is, in most cases, based on middleware. Middleware is also described as communication infrastructure.
- **Routing schemes**: Information can be routed in different ways within a network. Depending on the type of routing used, routing schemes can be broken down into **unicast** (1:1 relationship), **broadcast** (all destinations), **multicast** (1:N), and **anycast** (1:N — most accessible).

Basic Principles

A2A, B2B, and B2C

Nowadays, business information systems in the majority of organizations consist of an application and system landscape, which has grown gradually over time. The increasing use of standard software (packaged applications) means that information silos will continue to exist. IT, however, should provide end-to-end support for business processes. This support cannot, and must not, stop at the boundaries of new or existing applications. For this reason, integration mechanisms are needed, which bring together individual island solutions to form a functioning whole. This happens not only at the level of an individual enterprise or organization, but also across different enterprises, and between enterprises and their customers. At an organizational level, a distinction is made between A2A, B2B, and B2C integration (Pape 2006). This distinction is shown in the image below. Each type of integration places specific requirements on the methods, technologies, products, and tools used to carry out the integration tasks. For example, the security requirements of B2B and B2C integrations are different from those of an A2A integration.

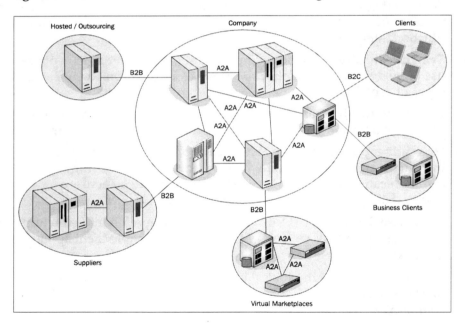

Modern concepts such as the **Extended Enterprise** integration across organizational boundaries, (Konsynski 1993) and the **Virtual Enterprise** (Hardwick, Bolton 1997) can be described using a combination of the different integration terms.

Integration types

Integration projects are generally broken down into information portals, shared data integration, and shared function integration. Portals integrate applications at a user interface level. Shared data integration involves implementing integration architectures at a data level, and shared function integration at a function level.

Information portals

The majority of business users need access to a range of systems in order to be able to run their business processes. They may need to be able to answer specific questions (that is, a call center taking incoming customer calls must be able to access the latest customer data) or to initiate or implement certain business functions (that is, updating customer data). In these circumstances, employees often have to use several business systems at the same time. An employee may need to access an order system (on a host) in order to verify the status of a customer order and, at the same time, may also have to open a web-based order system to see the data entered by the customer. Information portals bring together information from multiple sources. They display it in one place so that users do not have to access several different systems (which might also require separate authentication) and can work as efficiently as possible (Kirchhof et al. 2003). Simple information portals divide the user's screen into individual areas, each of which displays the data from one backend system independently, without interacting with the others. More sophisticated systems allow for limited interaction between the individual areas, which makes it possible to synchronize the different areas. For example, if the user selects a record in one area, the other areas are updated. Other portals use such advanced integration technology that the boundaries between the portal application and the integrated application become blurred (Nussdorfer, Martin 2006).

Shared data

Shared databases, file replication, and data transfers fall in the category of integration using shared data (Gorton 2006).

- **Shared databases**: Many different business systems need to access the same data. For example, customer addresses may be required in an order system, a CRM system, and a sales system. This kind of data can be stored in a shared database in order to reduce redundancy and synchronization problems.
- **File replication**: Systems often have their own local data storage. This means that any centrally managed data (in a top-level system) has to be replicated in the relevant target databases, and updated and synchronized regularly.
- **Data transfers**: Data transfers are a special form of data replication in which the data is transferred in files.

Shared business functions

In the same way that different business systems store redundant data, they also have a tendency to implement redundant business logic. This makes maintenance and adapting to new situations both difficult and costly. For example, different systems must be able to validate data using predefined, centrally managed business rules. It makes sense to manage such logic in a central place.

- **EAI**: The term EAI is generally used to describe all the methods which attempt to simplify the process of making a connection between different systems, in order to avoid a type of "spaghetti architecture" which results from the uncontrolled use of proprietary point-to-point connections. The systems are linked together with EAI solutions, instead of a single proprietary application programming interface (API).
- **SOA**: Service-oriented architecture is a term used to describe one way of implementing an enterprise architecture. SOA begins with an analysis of the business, in order to identify and structure the individual business areas and processes. This allows for the definition of services, which implement individual areas of business functionality. In an SOA, technical services are the equivalent of the specialist business areas, or functionality, in the business processes. This represents a major conceptual difference when compared with classic EAI solutions, which have a quite different focus. Their approach involves the simple exchange of data between systems, regardless of the technical semantics, and independently of any technical analysis of the processes.

Differences between EAI and SOA

In many cases, EAI solutions have only been able to fulfill the expectations placed on them to either a limited extent, or in an unsatisfactory way. This is, among other things, due to the following factors (Rotem-Gal-Oz 2007):

- EAI solutions are generally data oriented and not process oriented.
- EAI solutions do not address business processes. Instead, they are defined independently.
- EAI solutions are highly complex, and because of their use of proprietary technologies, do not allow for long-term protection of investments, which is possible when using open standards.
- EAI solutions need product-specific knowledge, which is only relevant in an EAI context, and cannot be reused in other projects.
- In the long term, EAI solutions are almost as costly to operate as the previously mentioned "home-made" spaghetti architectures.

If EAI solutions are used in combination with web services to link systems together, this is still not the equivalent of an SOA. Although the number of proprietary connection components between the systems being linked are reduced by the use of open **WS-*** standards, a "real" SOA involves a more extensive architectural approach, based on a (business) process-oriented perspective on integration problems.

While EAI is data driven and puts the emphasis on application interface integration, SOA is a (business) process-driven concept, which focuses on integrating service interfaces in compliance with open standards encapsulating the differences in individual integration approaches. As a result, it removes the barrier between the data integration and application integration approaches. However, SOA has one significant problem, which is that of semantic integration. Existing web services do not provide a satisfactory answer to this problem, but they do allow us to formulate the right questions in order to identify future solutions.

Semantic integration and the role of data

The challenge represented by semantic integration is based on the following problem:

- The representation of the data and the information contained in the data are often closely interlinked, and not separated into user data and metadata.
- The information suffers from the missing data context; there is no meta information defining how the data needs to be interpreted.

This means that the data structure and data information (its meaning) are often not the same thing and, therefore, have to be interpreted (Inmon, Nesavich 2008).

The following example will help to make this clearer:

A date, such as "7 August 1973," forms part of the data. It is not clear whether this information is a text string or in a date format. It may even be in another format and will have to be calculated on the basis of reference data before runtime. This information is of no relevance to the user.

However, it might be important to know what this date refers to, in other words, its semantic meaning in its reference context. Is it a customer's birthday, or the date on which a record was created? This example can even be more complex.

Another example that can be interpreted differently in different contexts is the term *Caesar*, for instance. Depending on the context, it could be the name of a pet or the name of pet food, a well-known salad, a gambling casino, or the name of a Roman emperor.

It is clear that data without a frame of reference is lacking any semantic information, causing the data to be ambiguous and possibly useless. Ontologically-oriented interfaces, as well as adaptive interfaces, can help to create such semantic reference and will become increasingly important in the field of autonomous B2B or B2C marketplaces in the future.

One semantic integration approach is, for example, the use of model-based semantic repositories (Casanave 2007). These repositories store and maintain implementation and integration designs for applications and processes (Yuan et al. 2006). They access existing vocabularies and reference models, which enable a standardized modeling process to be used. Vocabularies create a semantic coupling between data and specific business processes, and it is through these vocabularies that the services and applications involved are supplied with semantic information in the surrounding technical context. The primary objective of future architectures must be to maintain the glossary and the vocabularies, in order to create a common language and, therefore, a common understanding of all the systems and partners involved. Semantic gaps must be avoided or bridged wherever possible, for example transforming input and output data by using canonical models and standardized formats for business documents. These models and formats can be predefined for different industries as reference models [EDI (FIPS 1993), RosettaNet (Damodaran 2004), and so on]. Transformation rules can be generated and stored on the basis of reference models, in the form of data cards and transformation cards. In the future, there will be a greater focus on the declarative description (*what?*) and less emphasis on describing the concrete software logic (*how?*) when defining integration architectures. In other words, the work involved in integration projects will move away from implementation, and towards a conceptual description in the form of a generative approach, where the necessary runtime logic is generated automatically.

Enterprise Application Integration (EAI)

The term Enterprise Application Integration (EAI) has become popular with the increased importance of integration, and with more extensive integration projects. EAI is not a product or a specific integration framework, but can be defined as a combination of processes, software, standards, and hardware that allow for the end-to-end integration of several enterprise systems, and enable them to appear as a single system (Lam, Shankararaman 2007).

Definition of EAI
The use of EAI means the unrestricted sharing of data and business processes among any connected applications (Linthicum 2000).

From a business perspective, EAI can be seen as the competitive advantage that a company acquires when all its applications are integrated into one consistent information system. From a technical perspective, EAI is a process in which heterogeneous applications, functions, and data are integrated, in order to allow the shared use of data and the integration of business processes across all applications. The aim is to achieve this level of integration without major changes to the existing applications and databases, by using efficient methods that are cost and time effective.

In EAI, the focus is primarily on the technical integration of an application and system landscape. Middleware products are used as the integration tools, but, wherever possible, the design and implementation of the applications are left unchanged. Adapters enable information and data to be moved across the technologically heterogeneous structures and boundaries. The service concept is lacking, as well as the reduction of complexity and avoidance of redundancy offered by open standards. The service concept and the standardization only came later with the emergence of service-oriented architectures (SOA), which highlighted the importance of focusing on the functional levels within a company, and its business processes.

Nowadays, software products which support EAI are often capable of providing the technical basis for infrastructure components within an SOA. As they also support the relevant interfaces of an SOA, they can be used as the controlling instance for the orchestration, and help to bring heterogeneous subsystems together to form a whole. Depending on its strategic definition, EAI can be seen as a preliminary stage of SOA, or as a concept that competes with SOA.

SOA is now moving the concept of integration into a new dimension. Alongside the classic "horizontal" integration, involving the integration of applications and systems in the context of an EAI, which is also of importance in an SOA, SOA also focuses more closely on a "vertical" integration of the representation of business processes at an IT level (Fröschle, Reinheimer 2007).

SOAs are already a characteristic feature of the application landscape. It is advisable when implementing new solutions to ensure that they are SOA-compliant, even if there are no immediate plans to introduce an integration architecture, or an orchestration layer. This allows the transition to an SOA to be made in small, controllable steps, in parallel with the existing architecture and on the basis of the existing integration infrastructure.

Levels of integration

Integration architectures are based on at least three or four integration levels (after Puschmann, Alt 2004 and Ring, Ward-Dutton 1999):

- **Integration on data level**: Data is exchanged between different systems. The technology most frequently used for integration at data level is File Transfer Protocol (FTP). Another widespread form of data exchange is the direct connection of two databases. Oracle databases, for example, exchange data via database links or external tables.
- **Integration on object level**: Integration on object level is based on data-level integration. It allows systems to communicate by calling objects from outside the applications involved.
- **Integration on process level**: Integration on process level uses workflow management systems. At this level, communication between the different applications takes place through the workflows, which make up a business process.

Messaging

Message queues were introduced in the 1970s as a mechanism for synchronizing processes (Brinch Hansen 1970). Message queues allow for persistent messages and, therefore, for asynchronous communication and the guaranteed delivery of messages. Messaging decouples the producer and the consumer with the only common denominator being the queue.

The most important properties of messaging, quality attributes of messaging, are shown in the following table:

Attribute	Comment
Availability	Physical queues with the same logical name can be replicated across several server instances. In the case of a failure of one server, the clients can send the message to another.
Failure handling	If communication between a client and a server fails, the client can send the message via failover mechanisms to another server instance.

Attribute	Comment
Modifiability	Clients and servers are loosely coupled by the messaging concept, which means that they do not know each other. This makes it possible for both clients and servers to be modified without influencing the system as a whole. Another dependency between producer and consumer is the message format. This dependency can be reduced or removed altogether by introducing a self-descriptive general message format (**canonical** message format).
Performance	Messaging can handle several thousands of messages per second, depending on the size of the messages and the complexity of the necessary transformations. The quality of service also has a major influence on the overall performance. Non-reliable messaging, which involves no buffering provides better performance than reliable messaging, where the messages are stored (**persisted**) in the filesystem or in databases (local or remote), to ensure that they are not lost if a server fails.
Scalability	Replication and clustering make messaging a highly scalable solution.

Publish/subscribe

Publish/subscribe represents an evolution of messaging (Quema et al. 2002). A subscriber indicates, in a suitable form, its interest in a specific message or message type. The persistent queue guarantees secure delivery. The publisher simply puts its message in the message queue, and the queue distributes the message itself. This allows for many-to-many messaging:

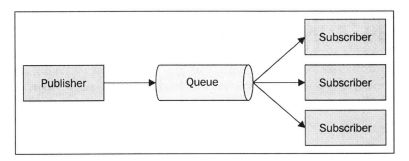

Basic Principles

The most important properties of publish/subscribe, quality attributes of publish/subscribe, are listed in the following table:

Attribute	Comment
Availability	Physical topics with the same logical name can be replicated across several server instances. In the case of the failure of one server, the clients can send the message to another.
Failure handling	In the case of the failure of one server, the clients can send the message to another replicated server.
Modifiability	The publisher and the subscriber are loosely coupled by the messaging concept, which means that they do not know each other. This makes it possible for both publisher and subscriber to be modified without influencing the system as a whole. Another dependency is the message format. This can be reduced or removed altogether by introducing a self-descriptive, general message format (canonical message format).
Performance	Publish/subscribe can process thousands of messages per second. Non-reliable messaging is faster than reliable messaging, because reliable messages have to be stored locally. If a publish/subscribe broker supports multicast/broadcast protocols, several messages can be transmitted to the subscriber simultaneously, but not serially.
Scalability	Topics can be replicated across server clusters. This provides the necessary scalability for very large message throughputs. Multicast/broadcast protocols can also be scaled more effectively than point-to-point protocols.

Message brokers

A message broker is a central component, which is responsible for the secure delivery of messages (Linthicum 1999). The broker has logical ports for receiving and sending messages. It transports messages between the sender and the subscriber, and transforms them where necessary.

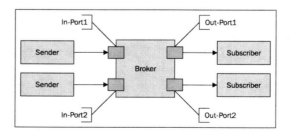

The most important tasks of a message broker, as shown in the preceding diagram, are implementing a hub-and-spoke architecture, the routing, and the transformation of messages.

- **Hub-and-spoke architecture**: The broker acts as a central message hub with the senders and receivers arranged like spokes around it. Connections to the broker are done through adapter ports that support the relevant message format.
- **Message routing**: The broker uses processing logic to route the messages. Routing decisions can be hardcoded, or can be specified in a declarative way. They are often based on the content of the message (content-based routing) or on specific values or attributes in the message header (attribute-based routing).
- **Message transformation**: The broker logic transforms the message input format into the necessary message output format.

The most important properties of a message broker, quality attributes of a message broker, are listed in the following table:

Attribute	Comment
Availability	To provide high availability, brokers must be replicated and operate in a clusters.
Failure handling	Brokers have different types of input ports that validate incoming messages to ensure that they have the correct format, and reject those with the wrong format. If one broker fails, the clients can send the message to another replicated broker.
Modifiability	Brokers separate transformation logic and routing logic from one another and from senders and receivers. This improves modifiability, as the logic has no influence on senders and receivers.
Performance	Because of the hub-and-spoke approach, brokers can potentially be a **bottleneck**. This applies in particular in the case of a high volume of messages, large messages and complex transformations. The throughput is typically lower than with simple reliable messaging.
Scalability	Broker clusters allow for high levels of scalability.

Messaging infrastructure

A messaging infrastructure provides mechanisms for sending, routing, and converting data, between different applications running on different operating systems with different technologies, as shown in the following diagram (Eugster et al. 2003):

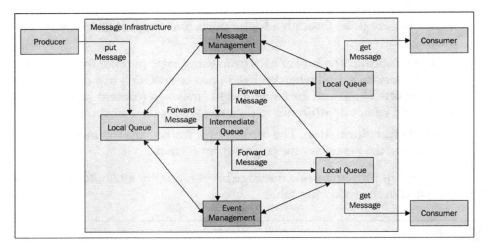

A messaging infrastructure involves the following parties/components:

- **Producer:** An application which sends messages to a local queue.
- **Consumer:** An application which is interested in specific messages.
- **Local queue**: The local interface of the messaging infrastructure. Each message sent to a local queue is received by the infrastructure and routed to one or more receivers.
- **Intermediate queue**: In order to ensure that messages are delivered, the infrastructure uses intermediate queues, in case a message cannot be delivered, or has to be copied for several receivers.
- **Message management**: Message management includes sending, routing, and converting data, together with special functions, such as guaranteed delivery, message monitoring, tracing individual messages, and error management.
- **Event management**: The subscription mechanism is controlled through special events.

Enterprise Service Bus

An Enterprise Service Bus is an infrastructure that can be used to implement an EAI. The primary role of the ESB is to decouple client applications from services, as shown in the following diagram (Chappell 2004):

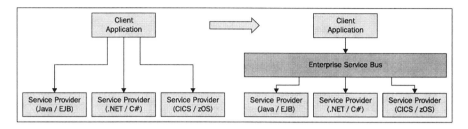

The encapsulation of services by the ESB means that the client application does not need to know anything about the location of the services, or the different communication protocols used to call them. The ESB enables the shared, enterprise-wide, and even intra-enterprise use of services and separate business processes from the relevant service implementations (Lee et al. 2003).

The core functions of an ESB

The major SOA vendors now offer specific Enterprise Service Bus products, which provide a series of core functions in one or another form, shown in the following diagram:

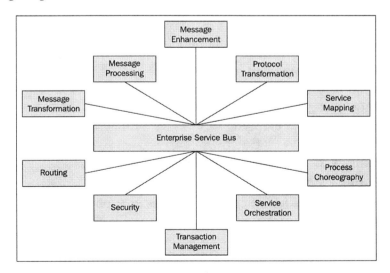

The structure of an ESB

The following diagram shows the basic structure of an ESB in a vendor-neutral way:

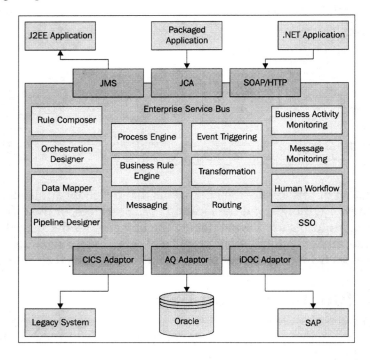

The naming for the single components used by the different vendors of SOA products will vary from those shown in the above diagram, but the products provide the following functions as a minimum (Craggs 2003):

- Routing and messaging as base services
- A communication bus, which enables a wide variety of systems to be integrated using predefined adapters
- Transformation and mapping services for a range of different conversions and transformations
- Mechanisms for executing processes and rules
- Monitoring functions for a selection of components
- Development tools for modeling processes, mapping rules, and message transfers
- A series of standardized interfaces, such as JMS (Java Messaging Specification (Hapner et al. 2002)), JCA (Java Connector Architecture (JCASpec 2003)), and SOAP/HTTP

Middleware

In most cases the technological realization of EAI systems is done through what is commonly termed **middleware**. Middleware is also described as a communication infrastructure. It allows communication between software components, regardless of the programming language in which the components were created, the protocols used for communication, and the platform on which the components are running (Thomson 1997). A distinction is made between the different types of middleware according to the methods of communication used, and the base technology.

Middleware communication methods

Communication methods for middleware can be broken down into five categories:

- **Conversational (Dialog-Oriented)**: The components interact synchronously with one another. They always react instantly to the information being exchanged. This type of communication is generally used in real-time systems.
- **Request/reply**: This is used when an application needs to call functions from another application. It corresponds to a call to a subroutine, with the important difference that the communication can take place over a network.
- **Message passing**: This enables information to be exchanged in a simple and well-directed way using messages. Communication takes place in one direction only. If an application wants to react to an incoming message, its response must be placed in another message.
- **Message queuing**: Information is exchanged in the form of messages which are sent through a queue, in other words, indirectly. Queuing allows the secure, planned, and prioritized delivery of messages. It is often used for the near real-time exchange of information between loosely coupled systems.
- **Publish/subscribe**: Two roles are involved in non-directed communication: the publisher of a message sends the message only to the middleware. The subscriber subscribes to all the types of message that are of interest to him or her. The middleware ensures that all subscribers receive the corresponding messages from a publisher.

Basic Principles

Middleware type	Communication	Relationship	Synchronous/ asynchronous	Interaction
Peer-to-peer, API	Conversational	1:1	Synchronous	Blocking
Database gateways	Request/reply	1:1	Synchronous	Blocking
Database replication	Request/reply/	1:N	Synchronous	Blocking
	Message queue	1:N	Asynchronous	Non-blocking
Remote procedure calls	Request/reply	1:1	Mostly synchronous	Mostly blocking
Object request brokers	Request/reply	1:1	Mostly synchronous	Mostly blocking
Direct messaging	Message passing	1:1	Asynchronous	Non-blocking
Message queue systems	Message queue	M:N	Asynchronous	Non-blocking
Message infrastructure	Publish/ subscribe	M:N	Asynchronous	Non-blocking

Middleware base technologies

Middleware can be broken down into the following base technologies:

- **Data-oriented middleware**: The integration or distribution of data to different RDBMS using the appropriate synchronization mechanisms.
- **Remote procedure call**: The implementation of the classic client/server approach.
- **Transaction-oriented middleware**: The transaction concept (ACID—Atomicity, Consistency, Isolation, Durability) is put into effect using this type of middleware. A transaction is a finite series of atomic operations which have either read or write access to a database.
- **Message-oriented middleware**: The information is exchanged by means of messages, which are transported by the middleware from one application to the next. Message queues are used in most cases.
- **Component-oriented middleware**: This represents different applications and their components as a complete system.

Routing schemes

Information can be routed in different ways within a network. Depending on the type of routing used, routing schemes can be broken down into the following four categories:

- Unicast (1:1 relationship)
- Broadcast (all destinations)
- Multicast (1:N)
- Anycast (1:N, most accessible)

Unicast

The unicast routing scheme sends data packages to a single destination. There is a 1:1 relationship between the network address and the network end point:

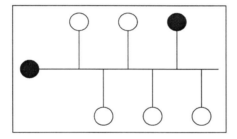

Broadcast

The broadcast routing scheme sends data packets in parallel to all the possible destinations in the network. If there is no support for this process, the data packets can be sent serially to all possible destinations. This produces the same results, but the performance is reduced. There is a 1:N relationship between the network address and the network end point.

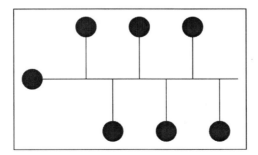

Multicast

The multicast routing scheme sends data packets to a specific selection of destinations. The destination set is a subset of all the possible destinations. There is a 1:N relationship between the network address and the network end point:

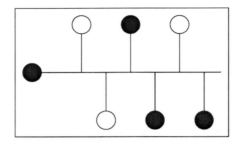

Anycast

The anycast routing scheme distributes information to the destination computer which is nearest, or most accessible. There is a 1:N relationship between the network address and the network end point, but only one end point is addressed at any given time for the purpose of routing the information.

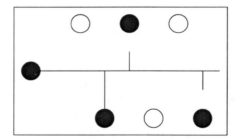

Integration architecture variants

The fundamental integration architecture variants are:

- **Point-to-point architecture**: A collection of independent systems which are connected through a network.
- **Hub-and-spoke architecture**: A further stage in the evolution of application and system integration, in which a central hub takes over responsibility for communications.

- **Pipeline architecture**: In pipeline architecture, independent systems along the value-added chain are integrated using a message bus. The bus capability results in the distribution of the interfaces to the central bus throughout the communication network, which gives applications a local access to a bus interface.
- **Service-oriented architecture**: The integration of different applications to form a functioning whole by means of distributed and independent service calls, which are orchestrated through an ESB and, if necessary, a Process Engine.

Point-to-point architecture

A point-to-point architecture is a collection of independent systems which are connected through a network. All the systems have equal rights, and can both use and provide services (Lublinsky 2002). This architecture can be found in many organizations, where application islands that have grown through time have been connected directly to each other.

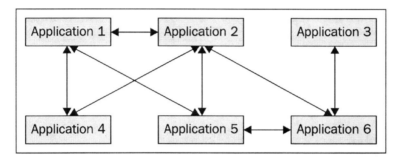

As shown in the above diagram, in this architecture, there is no central database—each system has its own data storage.

New systems are connected directly with the existing ones, which over time leads to a highly complex set of interfaces. A point-to-point architecture with n applications can in theory have $n*(n-1)/2$ interfaces.

It is easy to imagine how complex, error-prone, and difficult it can be to maintain such an architecture as more and more applications are added. Expanding the system is costly and, as the number of interfaces grows, operation becomes increasingly time consuming and expensive. A SWOT analysis is shown in the following table:

Strengths	Weaknesses
<ul><li>Low startup and infrastructure costs</li><li>Autonomous systems</li></ul>	<ul><li>Only practical if there are a few systems and a few connections</li><li>Replacing individual systems is a highly laborious and costly process</li><li>Very inflexible, not the base for an SOA and, therefore, it is difficult to represent business processes</li><li>No overview of data</li><li>Limited reusability of components</li><li>Time consuming and costly operation</li></ul>
Opportunities	**Threats**
<ul><li>Functions within the systems can be rapidly adapted to meet new requirements</li></ul>	<ul><li>High follow-up costs</li><li>Lack of standardization</li></ul>

Hub-and-spoke architecture

Hub-and-spoke architecture represents a further stage in the evolution of application and system integration, as shown in the following diagram (Gilfix 2003):

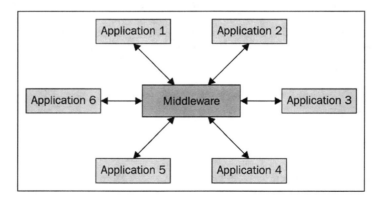

Its objective is to minimize the growing interface complexity by using a central integration platform to exchange messages between the systems. The central integration platform can transform messages, route them from one application to the next, and change the content of the messages. This architecture is often used for complex data distribution mechanisms. A SWOT analysis is shown in the following table:

Strengths	Weaknesses
<ul><li>Reduction of the interface problem</li><li>Low follow-up costs</li><li>Compliance with standards</li><li>Autonomous systems</li><li>Simplified monitoring</li></ul>	<ul><li>High startup and infrastructure costs</li></ul>
Opportunities	**Threats**
<ul><li>Individual systems can be integrated/replaced easily</li></ul>	<ul><li>With high transfer volumes, the central hub could become a performance bottleneck</li><li>Single point of failure</li></ul>

Pipeline architecture

In a pipeline architecture, independent systems along the value-added chain are integrated using a message bus, as in the following figure. The implementation of this architecture corresponds to that of the hub-and-spoke architecture, as the corresponding middleware products are normally installed and operated on central servers. The bus capability results in the distribution of the interfaces to the central bus throughout the communication network, which generally also gives applications local access to a bus interface (Ambriola, Tortora 1993).

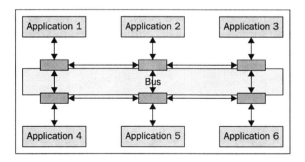

Similarly to the hub-and-spoke architecture, this architecture also keeps interface problems to a minimum. The use of appropriate middleware components allows the communication between the systems to be standardized. The bus system is responsible for message distribution. The transformation and routing rules are stored in a central repository. Depending on the middleware product in use, business functions and rules can also be represented. A SWOT analysis is shown in the following table:

Strengths	Weaknesses
<ul><li>Low follow-up costs</li><li>Very flexible architecture</li><li>Compliance with standards</li><li>Autonomous systems</li></ul>	<ul><li>High startup and infrastructure costs</li></ul>
Opportunities	**Threats**
<ul><li>Individual systems can be integrated/replaced easily</li></ul>	<ul><li>With high transfer volumes, there is the risk of a performance bottleneck, if it is not separated from normal traffic (for example, separate bulk channel)</li></ul>

This form of architecture is ideal for:

- Very high performance requirements (event-driven architecture)
- 1:N data distribution (for example, broadcasting)
- N:1 database (for example, data warehouse)

Service-oriented architecture

The core of a service-oriented architecture, and the main distinction between this form of architecture and those described earlier, is the fact that business processes and applications are no longer coded as complex program structures, but are orchestrated as independent, distributed service calls.

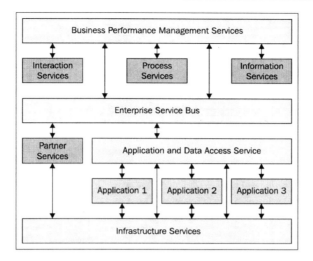

An ESB is used as the central integration component for service calls. It has similar properties to those of the integration platform in hub-and-spoke architecture, or of the bus in pipeline architecture. A SWOT analysis is shown in the following table

Strengths	Weaknesses
• Low follow-up costs • Very flexible architecture • Compliance with standards • Supported by all major software houses	• High startup and infrastructure costs • Requires a comprehensive SOA strategy and governance

Opportunities	Threats
• Individual systems can be implemented and orchestrated easily	• Lack of focus on relevant business processes

Patterns for EAI/EII

Three basic patterns are used for the implementation of EAI and EII platforms:

- Direct connection
- Broker
- Router

Direct connection

Direct connection represents the simplest type of interaction between two applications and is based on a 1: N topology, in other words, an individual point-to-point connection. It allows a pair of applications within an organization to communicate directly. Interactions between the source and the target applications can be as complex as necessary. Additional connection rules are defined for more complex point-to-point connections. Examples of connection rules include data mapping rules, security rules, and availability rules.

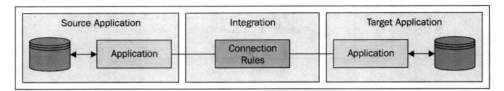

The direct connection pattern can be broken down into the following logical components:

- The source applications consist of one or more applications, which want to initiate interaction with the target applications.
- The connection is the line between the source and the target application, and represents a point-to-point connection between the two applications.
- Connection rules are the business rules which relate to the connection, such as data mapping and security rules.
- The target application is a new or existing (modified or unmodified) application, which provides the necessary business services.

The advantages and disadvantages of the direct connection pattern are shown in the following table:

Advantages	Disadvantages
• Functions well in the case of applications with simple integration requirements and only a few backend applications • Loose coupling • Receivers do not need to be online	• Results in several point-to-point connections between each pair of applications, and therefore, to spaghetti configurations • Does not support the intelligent routing of queries • Does not support the decomposition/re-composition of queries

Uses

Direct connection is used for the following purposes:

- Reducing the latency of business events
- Supporting the structured exchange of information within an organization
- Supporting real-time one-way message flows
- Supporting real-time request/reply message flows
- Continued use of legacy investments

Broker

The broker pattern is based on the direct connection pattern, and extends it to a 1: N topology. It allows an individual request from a source application to be routed to several target applications, which reduces the number of 1:1 connections required. The connection rules take the form of broker rules. This allows the distribution rules to be kept separate from the application logic (**Separation of Concerns** principle or **SoC**). The broker is also responsible for the composition and decomposition of interactions. The broker pattern uses the direct connection pattern for the connection between the applications. The broker pattern forms the base for the publish/subscribe message flow:

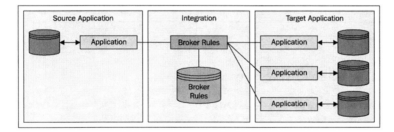

The broker pattern can be broken down into the following logical components:

- The source applications consist of one or more applications which want to interact with the target applications.
- The broker component keeps the number of direct connections to a minimum. It also supports message routing, message enhancement, and the transformation, decomposition, and re-composition of messages.
- The target applications consist of both new and existing (modified or unmodified) applications. These applications are responsible for implementing the necessary business services.

The advantages and disadvantages of the broker pattern are shown in the following table:

Advantages	Disadvantages
<ul><li>Allows for the interaction of several different applications.</li><li>Minimizes the impact on existing applications.</li><li>Makes routing services available, so that the source application no longer needs to know the target applications.</li><li>Provides transformation services, which enable the source and target applications to use different communication protocols.</li><li>Decomposition/re-composition services are available to allow a single request to be sent from one source to several target applications.</li><li>The use of the router keeps the number of necessary modifications to a minimum when the location of the target application is changed.</li></ul>	<ul><li>Logic has to be implemented on the broker for routing and decomposition/re-composition tasks.</li></ul>

Uses

Broker is used for the following purposes:

- An individual application should be able to interact with one or more target applications.
- A hub-and-spoke architecture reduces complexity when compared with a point-to-point architecture.
- The externalization of the routing, decomposition, and re-composition rules increases maintainability and flexibility.
- Broker pattern is important when a request is processed from a source application and results in several interactions with the target systems.
- The source system is decoupled from the target applications, and there is no dependency on the interfaces of these target applications.

Router

The router pattern is a variant of the broker pattern with several potential target applications, in which the message is always routed to only one target application. The router decides which target application will receive the interaction. While the broker pattern supports 1:N connections, the router pattern only allows 1:1 connections, as the router rules determine the target application in each case.

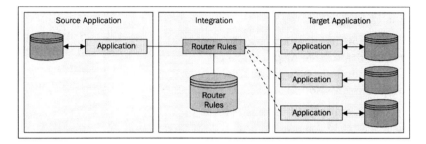

The router pattern as shown in the diagram can be broken down into the following logical components:

- The source applications consist of one or more applications that want to interact with the target applications.
- The router component provides all the business rules needed for processing the message, such as routing and transformation. It receives requests from several source applications, and routes them intelligently to the correct target application. The resulting integration is, in fact, a point-to-point connection between the source and the target.
- The target applications consist of both new and existing (modified or unmodified) applications. These applications are responsible for implementing the necessary business services.

Basic Principles

The advantages and disadvantages of the router pattern are shown in the following table:

Advantages	Disadvantages
• Allows for the interaction of several different applications. • Minimizes the impact on existing applications. • Makes routing services available, so that the source application no longer needs to recognize the target applications. • Provides transformation services which enable the source and target applications to use different communication protocols. • The use of the router keeps the number of necessary modifications to a minimum when the location of the target application is changed.	• No decomposition and re-composition of messages. • No possibility of sending several simultaneous requests to the target applications on the basis of the incoming request.

Uses

Router is used for the following purposes:

- An individual application should be able to interact with one of several target applications
- A hub-and-spoke architecture reduces complexity when compared with a point-to-point architecture
- The externalization of the routing, decomposition, and re-composition rules increases maintainability and flexibility
- Router pattern is important when a request is processed from a source application and results in an interaction with only one of several potential target systems
- As with the Broker pattern, the source system is also decoupled from the target applications, and has no dependency on the interfaces of these applications

Patterns for data integration

Data integration is implemented using three fundamental patterns:

- Federation
- Population
- Synchronization

Federation

The federation pattern is a simple data integration pattern that provides access to different data sources, and gives the calling application the impression that these sources are a single, logical data source. This is achieved as follows:

1. Expose a single consistent interface to the application.
2. Translate the interface to whatever interface is needed for the underlying data.
3. Compensate for any differences in function between the different data sources.
4. Allow data from different sources to be combined into a single result set that is returned to the user.

This is illustrated in the following diagram:

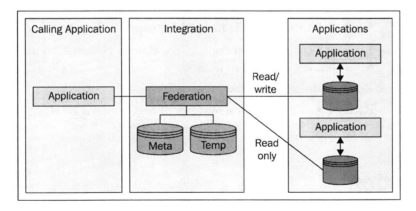

The federation pattern as shown in this diagram can be broken down into the following logical building blocks:

- The calling applications have the need for information, but they don't possess the information.

- The federation building block uses metadata to determine where the data required is stored, and in what format. The metadata repository allows the decomposition of a single query executed against the federation building block, into individual requests to different data sources. To the user (the calling application), the information model appears to be a single virtual repository. The data is accessed via suitable adapters for each target repository. The federation component sends an individual result to the calling application, and integrates several different formats into a shared federated schema.
- The source applications have the information that is important for the calling applications.

The federation pattern supports structured and unstructured data, together with read-only and read/write accesses to the underlying data sources. Read/write accesses should be limited, wherever possible, to a single data source, as otherwise a two-phase commit is needed, which can be difficult in distributed databases.

Uses

Federation is used for the following purposes:

- The data needed by an application is distributed across different databases (for historic, technical, or organizational reasons)
- Federation is more effective than other data integration technologies, when:
    - Near real-time access is needed for rapidly changing data
    - Making a consolidated copy of the data is not possible for technical, legal, or other reasons
    - Read/write access must be possible
    - Reducing or limiting the number of copies of the data is a goal
- It is possible to continue to make use of existing investments

Population

The population pattern has a very simple model. It gathers data from one or more data sources, processes the data in an appropriate way, and applies it to a target database. In its simplest form, the population pattern is based on the read dataset-process data-write dataset model. This corresponds to the classic ETL (Extract, Transform, and Load process.

This is illustrated in the following diagram:

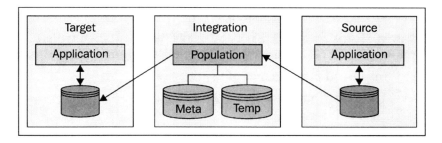

The population pattern can be broken down into the following logical components:

- The target applications have a need for information, which they do not possess. Therefore, a copy from another data source in a source application is required.
- The population component reads one or more data sources in the source application, and writes the data to a data source in the target application. The rules for extracting data from the source application can be as complex as necessary. They range from simple rules, such as *read all data*, to more complex rules where only specific fields in specific records can be read under certain conditions. The loading rules for the target database can vary from a simple overwrite of the data, to a more complex process of inserting new records and updating existing ones. The metadata is used to describe these rules.
- The source applications have the important information needed by the target applications.

Uses

Population is used for the following purposes:

- A specialized copy of existing data (derived data) is needed:
    - Subsets of existing data sources
    - A modified version of an existing data source
    - Combinations of existing data sources
- Only read access to the derived data in the target application is possible (or only a few write accesses).
- In the case of a significant number of write accesses, the two-way synchronization pattern should be used.

- The user must be provided with quick access to the information required, instead of being bombarded with too much, irrelevant, incorrect, or otherwise useless misinformation.
- However, IT drivers often dictate the use of the population pattern. In other words, the copies of data are made for technical reasons. These drivers include:
  - Improved performance of user access
  - Load distribution across systems

Synchronization

The synchronization pattern (also known as the **replication** pattern) enables bidirectional update flows of data in a multi-copy database environment. The "two-way" synchronization aspect of this pattern is what distinguishes it from the "one-way" capabilities provided by the population pattern.

This is illustrated in the following diagram:

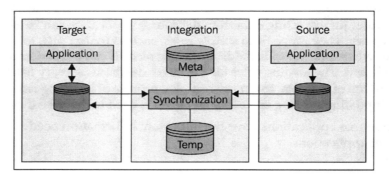

The synchronization pattern shown in this diagram can be broken down into the following logical components:

- The target applications have a need for information, which they do not possess. Therefore, a copy from another data source in a source application is required.
- At a simplistic level, the synchronization component can be compared to the population pattern, with the only difference being that the data flows in both directions. If the data elements flowing in both directions are fully independent, then two-way synchronization is no more than two separate instances of the population pattern. However, it is more common to find some overlap between the datasets flowing in either direction. In this case, conflict detection and resolution are needed.

- The source applications have information which is relevant to the target applications.

Uses

Synchronization is used for the following purpose:

- A specialized copy of existing data (derived data) is needed. This copy can take different forms:
    - Subsets of existing data sources
    - A modified version of an existing data source
    - Combinations of existing data sources

Multi-step synchronization

There is one variant of the synchronization pattern: the multi-step variant. The multi-step variant of the two-way synchronization pattern makes use of one instance of the population pattern, with its gather, process, and apply functions, for each of the two synchronization directions. An additional "reconcile" function is placed between the two data flows, and guarantees that there are no conflicts in the updates. If the opportunities for conflicts are minimal, this pattern can be constructed from existing population components. However, a specialized solution should be used for more complex situations.

The following diagram illustrates the "reuse" of the population pattern, once for each direction with the additional "reconcile" component in the middle.

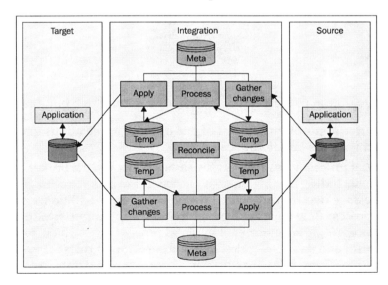

Basic Principles

Patterns for service-oriented integration

Service-oriented integration is based on two fundamental patterns:

- **Process integration**: The process integration pattern extends the 1: N topology of the broker pattern. It simplifies the serial execution of business services, which are provided by the target applications.
- **Workflow integration**: This is basically a variant of the serial process pattern. It extends the capability of simple serial process orchestration to include support for user interaction during the execution of individual process steps.

Process integration

The process integration pattern extends the 1: N topology of the broker pattern seen in EAI. It simplifies the serial execution of business services, which are provided by the target applications, and therefore enables the orchestration of serial business processes, based on the interaction of the source application. The serial sequence is defined using process rules, which allows for decoupling from the process logic (flow logic and the domain logic) of the individual application. The rules define not only the control and data flow, but also the permitted call rules for each target application. Interim results (process data) are stored in individual results databases.

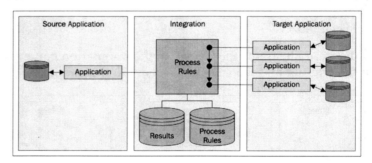

The process integration pattern can be broken down into three building blocks:

- The source applications consist of one or more applications that want to interact with the target applications.
- The serial process rules support the same services as the broker in the broker pattern, including routing queries, protocol conversion, message broadcasting, and message decomposition and re-composition. In addition, externalization of the process flow logic from the individual applications is also supported. The process logic is determined by serial process rules which, together with the control and data flow rules, define the execution rules for each target application. These rules are stored in a process rules database.

- The target applications consist of both new and existing (modified or unmodified) applications. These applications are responsible for implementing the necessary business services.

The advantages and disadvantages of the process integration pattern are shown in the following table:

Advantages	Disadvantages
• Improves the flexibility and responsiveness of an organization by implementing end-to-end process flows and externalizing process logic from individual applications. • Provides a foundation for Business Process Management that enables the effectiveness of business processes to be monitored and measured.	• Only direct, automatic processing supported. No user interaction is possible (refer to the workflow variant). • No parallel processing possible.

Uses

Process integration is used for the following reasons:

- Support for end-to-end process flows which use the services provided by the target applications
- Improves the flexibility and responsiveness of IT by externalizing process logic from individual applications

Variants

There are two variants of this pattern:

The **parallel process** pattern extends the simple serial process orchestration provided by the serial process patterns, by supporting concurrent execution and orchestration of business service calls. The concurrent execution of sub-processes requires the sub-steps to be split up and brought together, so that they can be executed in parallel. Different patterns are available for this purpose at an implementation level (for example, patterns for parallel computing and different architecture styles (for example, pipes-and-filters architectures). The interim results of a sub-step may or may not influence the overall results. It is also possible for the interim results of a sub-step to influence the execution of other sub-steps.

The **external business rules** variant adds the option of externalizing business rules from the serial process, into a business rule engine, where they can be evaluated. The process only reacts to the responses of the rule engine. The complex rule evaluations are carried out by the specialized rule engine. Externalizing the rules improves flexibility and responsiveness, because the business rules can be adapted much more easily and quickly.

Workflow integration

The workflow integration pattern represents an extension of the process integration pattern, as illustrated in the following diagram:

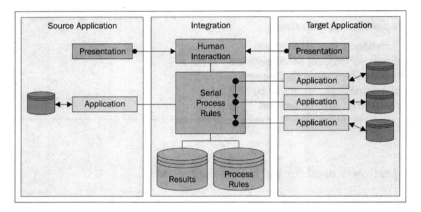

It extends the capability of simple serial process orchestration to include support for user interaction during the execution of individual process steps. As a result, it supports a classic workflow.

Variants

The **parallel workflow** integration pattern is a variant of the workflow integration pattern, and corresponds to the parallel process integration pattern which forms part of the process integration pattern. It extends the capability of **parallel process orchestration** to include support for user interaction during the execution of individual process steps. As a result, it supports a parallel workflow.

Event-driven architecture

Event-driven architecture (EDA) is one of the hot topics of the industry. These architectures are often wrongly referred to as the successors to SOAs (Mühl et al. 2006). In fact, the concepts involved in EDA are as old as IT itself. In addition, EDAs are growing rapidly in popularity, together with the integration architectures of SOA. However, both types of architecture can be used completely independently of one another, and can be combined orthogonally. From the perspective of integration, two aspects of EDA are of particular interest:

- The symbiosis between EDA and SOA that has already been referred to, which allows SOA domains to be linked/integrated together on an event-driven basis.
- The technology offered by EDA which enables events from one or more event streams on the data integration level to be consolidated into new information.

Introducing EDA

According to a study by Gartner (Gartner 2006), the success of companies such as Dell and Google is due to the fact that these organizations are able to identify market factors or market events in the global marketplace at an early stage, and follow them up consistently and quickly. Both examples are very close to the picture drawn by Gartner of an ideal organization: the **real-time enterprise** (**RTE**). An RTE is characterized by its highly-automated business processes and the shortest possible process runtimes (Nussdorfer, Martin 2003).

Basic Principles

While SOA concepts within IT structures form the basis for the automation of business processes, the second step, which relates to the ideal image of the RTE, involves processing more fine-grained information about changes in the state of these business processes. The complexity of these state changes is increasing noticeably, in the same way that the number of reaction interfaces in the business processes is. This is where the significance of EDA lies, because the observable changes in the state of the business processes can be modeled as events. Classic integration architectures, such as **OLTP (Online Transaction Processing)**) or **OLAP (Online Analytical Processing)** are no longer able to meet the requirements for rapid and consistent action on the basis of event analyses (Zeidler 2007).

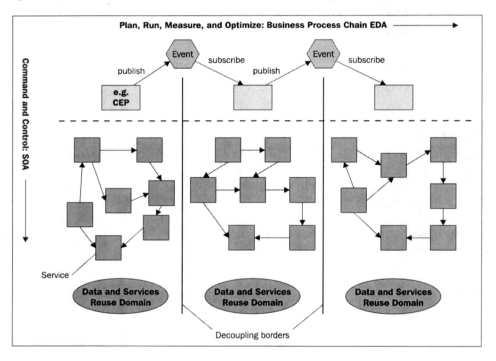

The above diagram illustrates the symbiosis between EDA and SOA, which is often referred to as **SOA 2.0** (Carter 2007) or **Next Generation SOA** (Luckham 2002). An SOA or an SOA domain provides the technical services, independently of consumers. These services can be combined or orchestrated, and they form the building blocks for the business processes. If a service of this kind triggers an event, for example because of a change in its state, an orthogonal EDA extension can activate a new SOA domain. As a result, a service becomes an event-producing building block in an EDA. In contrast to the typical producer/consumer patterns of an SOA, the EDA largely uses a publish/subscribe mechanism. An event processor processes the events as they occur, and publishes the processed results via an event channel, which triggers the services of other SOA domains. Various types of event processor are used depending on the type of event processing required. These include **Complex Event Processors (CEP)**, for example, which are described later in this chapter.

The SOA domains (to be integrated) should ideally be defined in such a way that they represent reusable services which can be used several times in business process chains of any length. The principle of loose coupling for the formation of such flexible business process chains is of decisive importance in the EDA, in the same way as it is in the SOA.

Event processing

The second aspect of integration that we want to highlight is of a more technical nature. It concerns the possibilities for event processing within an EDA concept, as shown in the following figure:

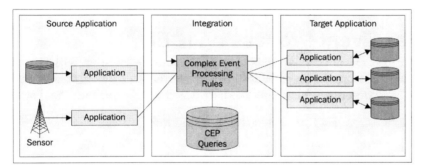

Event-processing technologies have been in day-to-day use in many industries for several years. Examples include algorithmic trading in stock markets and **Radio Frequency Identification (RFID)** in road charging systems.

There are three fundamental types of event processing:

- **Simple Event Processing (SEP)**
- **Event Stream Processing (ESP)**
- **Complex Event Processing (CEP)**

Simple Event Processing (SEP)

Events occur either individually, or in streams. Single events can be regarded as an important change in state in a message source and, in particular, in a business event. Events of this kind typically trigger processes in the systems which receive the message. This form of event processing corresponds exactly with the specification of the **Java Messaging Service (JMS)**. Therefore, a typical example of SEP is JMS.

Event Stream Processing (ESP)

ESP involves processing streams of incoming messages or events. Typical ESP systems have sensors which channel a large number of events, and use filters and other processing methods to influence the stream of messages or events. Individual events are less important, and instead the focus is on the event stream. Well-known examples include the systems which track stock market prices: one single fluctuation in prices is generally not particularly significant. A more informative overall trend can only be determined from several events.

Complex Event Processing (CEP)

The third form of event processing is Complex Event Processing, which is part of ESP. In CEP there is a strong focus on identifying patterns in a large number of events and their (message) contents, which may be distributed across different data streams.

The CEP funnel model is illustrated in the following figure:

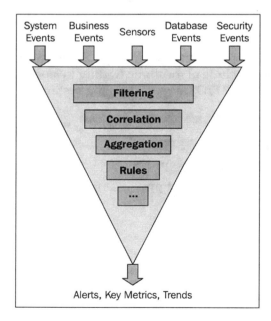

The CEP funnel model illustrates the process of compressing (large) volumes of events to produce compressed information. The source of the events includes business events (Viehmann 2008). One of the classic uses of CEP is in tracing credit card fraud. In the case of two transactions using the same credit card, which were made within a short period of time, in locations a long distance apart, this type of geographical and chronological pattern indicating the possibility of fraud, can easily be applied to the model. Systems of this kind, which correlate thousands of events in order to filter out the few cases of fraud or misbehavior, are more and more frequently in use.

Grid computing/Extreme Transaction Processing (XTP)

Grid computing and XTP are the new integration technologies, which are likely to become increasingly popular over the next few years.

- **Grid computing**: An infrastructure for the integrated, collaborative use of resources. Grids can be broken down into Data Grids, In-Memory Data Grids, Domain Entity Grids, and Domain Object Grids on the basis of their primary functionality, and are used in a wide range of applications.
- **XTP**: This is a distributed storage architecture, which allows for parallel application access. It is designed for distributed access to large, and very large, volumes of data.

Grid computing

Grid computing is the term used to describe all the methods that combine the computing power of a number of computers in a network, in a way that enables the (parallel) solution of compute-intensive problems (distributed computing), in addition to the simple exchange of data. Every computer in the grid is equal to all the others. Grids can exceed the capacity and the computing power of today's super computers at considerably lower cost, and are also highly scalable. The computing power of the grid can be increased by adding computers to the grid network, or combining grids to create meta grids.

Definition of a grid

A grid is an infrastructure enabling the integrated, collaborative use of resources which are owned and managed by different organizations (Foster, Kesselmann 1999).

The following diagram illustrates the basic model of grid computing, with the network of computers forming the grid in the middle:

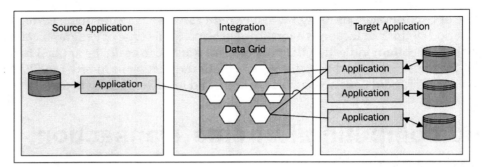

The main tasks of grids are:

- **Distributed caching and processing**: Data is distributed across all the nodes in a grid. Different distribution topologies and strategies are available for this purpose. A data grid can be divided into separate sub-caches, which allows for the use of more effective access mechanisms involving pre-filtering. The distribution of the data across different physical nodes guarantees the long-term availability and integrity of the data, even if individual nodes fail. Automatic failover behavior and load balancing functionality are part of the grid infrastructure. Transaction security is also guaranteed throughout the entire grid.
- **Event-driven processing**: The functionality of computational grids. Computing operations and transactions can take place in parallel across all the nodes in a grid. Simple event processing, similar to the trigger mechanism of databases, ensures that it is possible for the system to react to data changes. Individual pieces of data in the grid can be joined together to form more complex data constructs using the "in-memory views" and "in-memory materialized views" concepts.

Grids have the following features which allow more sophisticated **Service Level Agreements (SLA)** to be set up:

- Predictable scalability
- Continuous availability
- Provision of a replacement connection in the case of a server failure (failover)
- Reliability

Grids can be broken down into data grids, in-memory data grids, domain entity grids, and domain object grids on the basis of their primary functionality.

Data grids

A data grid is a system made up of several distributed servers which work together as a unit to access shared information and run shared, distributed operations on the data.

In-memory data grids

In-memory data grids are a variant of data grids in which the shared information is stored locally in memory in a distributed (often transactional) cache. A distributed cache is a collection of data or, more accurately, a collection of objects that is distributed (or partitioned) across any number of cluster nodes, in such a way that exactly one node in the cluster is responsible for each piece of data in the cache, and the responsibility is distributed among the cluster nodes.

Competitive data accesses are handled cluster-wide by the grid infrastructure, if a specific transactional behavior is required. The advantages include the high levels of performance possible as a result of low latency memory access. Today's 64-bit architectures and low memory prices allow larger volumes of data to be stored in memory where they are available for low latency access.

However, if the memory requirements exceed the memory available, "overflow" strategies can be used to store data on a hard disk (for example, in the local filesystem or local databases). This will result in a drop in performance caused by higher latency. The latest developments, such as solid state disks, will in future allow a reasonable and cost-effective compromise in this area, and will be an ideal solution in scenarios of this kind.

Data loss caused by a server failing and, therefore, its area of the memory being lost, can be avoided by the redundant distribution of the information. Depending on the product, different distribution topologies and strategies can be selected or enhanced.

In the simplest case, the information is distributed evenly across all the available servers.

An in-memory data grid helps the application to achieve shorter response times by storing the user data in memory in formats which are directly usable by the application. This ensures that storage accesses with low latency and complex, time-consuming transformations and aggregations when the consumer accesses the data can be avoided. Because the data in the grid is replicated, buffering can be used to accommodate database failures, and the availability of the system is improved. If a cluster node in the data grid fails, the data is still available on at least one other node, which also increases availability. Data will only be lost in the case of a total failure, and this can be counteracted by regular buffering to persistent storage (hard disk, solid state disk, and so on).

Domain entity grids

Domain entity grids distribute the domain data of the system (the applications) across several servers. As these are often coarse granular modules with a hierarchical structure, their data may have to be extracted from several different data sources before being made available on the grid across the entire cluster. The data grid takes on the role of an aggregator/assembler which gives the consumers cluster-wide, high-performance access to the aggregated entities. The performance can be further improved by the grid by initializing the domain data before it is actually used (pre-population).

Domain object grids

A domain object grid distributes the runtime components of the system (the applications) and their status (process data) across a number of servers. This may be necessary for reasons of fail-safety, and also because of the parallel execution of program logic. By adding additional servers, applications can be scaled horizontally. The necessary information (data) for the parallelized functions can be taken from shared data storage, (although this central access can become a bottleneck, which reduces the scalability of the system as a whole) or directly from the same grid or a different grid. It is important to take into account the possibilities of individual products or, for example, to combine several products (data grid and computing grid).

Distribution topologies

Different distribution topologies and strategies are available, such as replicated caches and partitioned caches (Misek, Purdy 2006).

Replicated caches

Data and objects are distributed evenly across all the nodes in the cluster. However, this means that the available memory of the smallest server acts as the limiting factor. This node determines how large the available data volume can be.

Advantages:

- The maximum access performance is the same across all the nodes, as all the nodes access local memory, which is referred to as **zero latency access**.

Disadvantages:

- Data distribution across all the nodes involves high levels of network traffic, and is time consuming. The same applies to data updates, which must be propagated across all the nodes.
- The available memory of the smallest server determines the capacity limit. This node places a limit on the size of the available data volume.

- In the case of transactionality, if a node is locked, every node must agree.
- In the case of a cluster error, all the stored information (data and locks) can be lost.

The disadvantages must be compensated for as far as possible by the grid infrastructure, and circumvented by taking appropriate measures. This should be made transparent to the programmer by using an API which is as simple as possible. The implementation could take the form of local read-only accesses without notification to the other cluster nodes. Operations with supervised competitive access require communication with at least one other node. All the cluster nodes must be notified about update operations. An implementation of this kind results in very high performance and scalability, together with transparent failover and failback.

However, it is important to take into consideration that replicated caches requiring a large number of data updates do not scale linearly in the case of potential cluster growth (adding nodes), which involves additional communication activities for each node.

Partitioned caches

Partitioned caches resolve the disadvantages of replicated caches, relating to memory and communications.

If this distribution strategy is used, several factors must be taken into account:

- **Partitioned**: The data is distributed across the cluster in such a way that there are no overlaps of responsibility with regard to data ownership. One node is solely responsible for a specific part of the data, and holds it as a master dataset. Among other things, this brings the benefit that the size of the available memory and computing power increases linearly as the cluster grows. In addition, compared with replicated caches, it has the advantage that all the operations which are carried out on the stored objects require only a single network hop. In other words, in addition to the server that manages the master data, only one other server needs to be involved, and this stores the accompanying backup data in the case of a failover. This type of access to master and backup data is highly scalable, because it makes the best possible use of point-to-point connections in a switched network.

- **Load-balanced**: Distribution algorithms ensure that the information in the cache is distributed in the best possible way across the available resources in the cluster, and therefore provide transparent load balancing (for the developer). In many products, the algorithms can be configured or replaced by in-house strategy modules. However, depending on the distribution and optimization strategy, this approach also has disadvantages. The dynamic nature of data distribution may cause data to be redistributed when the optimization strategy is activated, if another member is added to the cluster. In particular, in environments where temporary cluster members are highly volatile, frequent recalculations of the optimum distribution characteristics, and physical data redistribution with its accompanying network traffic, should be avoided. This can be achieved by identifying volatile cluster nodes within the grid infrastructure, and ensuring that they are not integrated into distribution strategies.
- **Location transparency**: Although the information about the nodes in the cluster is distributed, the same API is used to access it. In other words, the programmer's access to the information is transparent. He does not need to know where the information is physically located in the cluster. The grid infrastructure is responsible for adapting the data distribution as effectively as possible to access behavior. Heuristics, configurations, and exchangeable strategies are used for this purpose. As long as no specific distribution strategy needs to be created, the way in which the strategy functions in the background is unimportant.

Agents

Agents are autonomous programs that are triggered by an application, and are executed on the information stored in the grid under the control of the grid infrastructure. Depending on the product, specific classes of programming APIs may need to be extended or implemented for this purpose. Alternatively, declarative options allow agent functionality of this kind to be established (for example, using aspect-oriented methods or pre-compilation steps). Predefined agents are often provided with particular products.

Execution patterns

Let's take a brief look at these execution patterns:

- **Targeted execution**: Agents can be executed on one specific set of information in the data grid. The information set is identified using a unique key. It is the responsibility of the grid infrastructure to identify the best location in the cluster for the execution, on the basis of the runtime data available (for example, load ratios, node usage, network loads).

- **Parallel execution**: Agents can be executed on a specific group of information sets, which are identifiable by means of a number of unique keys. As with the target execution, it's the responsibility of the grid infrastructure to identify the best location in the cluster for the execution, on the basis of the runtime data available (for example, load ratios, node usage, network loads).
- **Query-based execution**: This is an extension of the parallel execution pattern. The number of information sets involved is not specified by means of the unique keys, but by formulating one or more filter functions in the form of a query object.
- **Data-grid-wide execution**: Agents are executed in parallel on all the available information sets in the grid. This is a specialized form of the query-based execution pattern in which a NULL query object is passed, in other words, a non-exclusive filter condition.
- **Data grid aggregation**: In addition to the scalar agents, cluster-wide aggregations can be run on the target data, so that computations can be carried out in (near) real-time. Products often provide predefined functionality for this purpose, including count, average, max, min, and so on.
- **Node-based execution**: Agents can be executed on specific nodes in the grid. An individual node can be specified. However, agents can also be run on a defined subset of the available nodes, or on all the nodes in the grid.

Uses

Grid technology can be used in a variety of different ways in architectures:

- **Distributed, transactional data cache (domain entities)**: Application data can be stored in a distributed cache in a linear scalable form, and with transactional access.
- **Distributed, transactional object cache (domain objects)**: Application objects (business objects) can be stored in a distributed cache in a linear scalable form and with transaction security.
- **Distributed, transactional process cache (process status)**: Process objects and their status can be stored in a distributed cache in a linear scalable form, and with transaction security.
- **SOA grid**: This is a specialized form of the previous scenario. **Business Process Execution Language (BPEL)** processes are distributed in serialized form (hydration) throughout the cluster, and can be processed further on another server following de-serialization (dehydration). This results in highly scalable BPEL processes.

- **Data access virtualization**: Grids allow virtualized access to distributed information in a cluster. As already mentioned, the location of the data is transparent during the access, regardless of the size of the cluster, which can also change dynamically.

- **Storage access virtualization**: Information is stored in a distributed cache in the format appropriate for the application, regardless of the type of source system and its access protocols or access APIs. This is particularly advantageous in cases where the information has to be obtained from distributed, heterogeneous source systems.

- **Data format virtualization**: Information is stored in a distributed cache in the format appropriate for the application, regardless of the formats in the source system. This is particularly advantageous in cases where the information has to be obtained from distributed, heterogeneous source systems.

- **Data access buffers**: The access to data storage systems (such as RDBMSs) is encapsulated and buffered so that it is transparent for the application. This allows any failover actions by the target system (for example, Oracle RAC) and the necessary reactions of the application to be decoupled. As a result, applications no longer need to be able to react to failover events on different target systems, as this takes place at grid level.

- **Maintenance window virtualization**: As already described, data grids support dynamic cluster sizing. Servers can be added to and removed from the cluster at runtime. This makes it possible to migrate distributed applications gradually, without significant downtimes for the application, or even the entire grid. A server can be removed from the cluster, the application can be migrated to this server, and the server can then be returned to the cluster. This process can be repeated with every other server. Applications developed in future on the basis of open standards will reduce this problem.

- **Distributed master data management**: In high-load environments, unacceptable bottlenecks may occur in central master data applications. Classic data replication can help to resolve this problem. However, it does involve the use of resources, and is not suitable for (near) real-time environments. Another solution is to distribute the master data across a data grid, provided that there is enough storage.

- **High performance backup and recovery**: It is possible to perform long-running backups in several stages in order to improve performance. The data can be written in stages to an in-memory cache, and then at delayed intervals to persistent storage.

- **Notification service in an ESB**: Grid technology replaces the message-based system used for notification in a service bus.

- **Complex real-time intelligence**: This combines the functionality of CEP and data grids, and therefore enables highly scalable analysis applications which provide complex pattern recognition functions in real-time scenarios, to be made available to the business. In its simplest form, this is an event-driven architecture with CEP engines as consumers, in which the message transport and the pre-analysis and pre-filtering of fine granular individual events is based on grid technology. The infrastructure components of the grid are also responsible for load balancing, fail-safety, and the availability of historic data from data marts in the in-memory cache. The combination of a grid and CEP makes it possible to provide highly scalable, but easily maintained, analysis architectures for (near) real-time business information.

XTP (Extreme Transaction Processing)

As a result of the need for complex processing of large and very large volumes of data (for example, in the field of XML, importing large files with format transformations, and so on.), new distributed storage architectures with parallel application access functions have been developed in recent years.

A range of different cross-platform products and solutions is available, also known as "extreme transaction processing" or XTP. The term was coined by the Gartner Group, and describes a style of architecture which aims to allow for secure, highly scalable and high-performance transactions across distributed environments on commodity hardware and software.

Solutions of this kind are likely to play an increasingly important role in service-oriented and event-driven architectures in the future. Interoperability is a driving force behind XTP.

Distributed caching mechanisms and grid technologies with simple access APIs form the basis for easy, successful implementation (in contrast to the complex products widely used in scientific environments in the past). Although distributed cache products already play a major role in "high-end transaction processing" (an expression coined by Forrester Research), their position in the emerging **Information-as-a-Service (IaaS)** market is expected to become more prominent.

New strategies for business priority have been introduced by financial service providers in recent years. Banks are attempting to go beyond the limits of their existing hardware resources and develop increasingly high-performance applications, without having to invest in an exponential increase of their hardware and energy costs.

Basic Principles

The growth of XTP in areas such as fraud detection, risk computation, and stock trade resolution is pushing existing systems to their performance limits. New systems which should implement this challenging functionality require new architecture paradigms.

It is clear that SOA, coupled with EDA and XTP, represents the future for financial service infrastructures as a means of achieving the goal of running complex computations with very large volumes of data, under real-time conditions. XTP belongs to a special class of applications (extreme transaction processing platforms) that need to process, aggregate, and correlate large volumes of data while providing high performance and high throughput. Typically, these processes produce large numbers of individual events that must be processed in the form of highly volatile data. XTP-style applications ensure that transactions and computations take place in the application's memory, and do not rely on complex remote accesses to backend services, in order to avoid communication latency (low latency computation). This allows for extremely fast response rates while still maintaining the transactional integrity of the data.

The SOA grid (next generation, grid-enabled SOA) is a conceptual variant of the XTPP (Extreme Transaction Processing Platform). It provides state-aware, continuous availability for service infrastructures, application data, and process logic. It is based on an architecture that combines horizontally scalable, database-independent, middle-tier data caching with intelligent parallelization, and brings together process logic and cache data for low latency (data and process affinity). This enables the implementation of newer, simpler, and more efficient models for highly scalable, service-oriented applications that can take full advantage of the possibilities of event-driven architectures.

XTP and CEP

XTP and CEP are comparable, in that they both consume and correlate large amounts of event data to produce meaningful results.

Often, however, the amount of event data that needs to be captured and processed far exceeds the capacity of conventional storage mechanisms ("there just isn't a disk that can spin fast enough"). In these cases, the data can be stored in a grid. CEP engines can be distributed across this data and can access it in parallel. Analyses can be carried out, and business event patterns can be identified and analyzed in real-time. These patterns can then be processed further and evaluated using **Business Activity Monitoring (BAM)**.

Solid State Disks and grids

Solid State Disk (SSD) technology is developing at high speed. Data capacities are increasing rapidly and compared with conventional drives, the I/O rates are phenomenal. Until now, the price/performance ratio per gigabyte of storage has been the major obstacle to widespread use. It is currently a factor of 12 of the cost of a normal server disk, per gigabyte of storage. The major benefit for data centers is the very low energy consumption, which is significantly less than that of conventional disks.

Because of their low energy requirements, high performance, low latency, and the expectation of falling costs, SSDs are an attractive solution in blades or dense racks. One interesting question concerns the influence which SSDs may have on data grid technology.

Disk-based XTP systems can benefit from the introduction of an SSD drive However, SSDs currently have a much lower storage capacity (128 GB versus 1 TB) than conventional disks. Nevertheless, this is more than the capacity of standard main memory, and SSDs are also less costly per gigabyte than memory. The capacity of SSDs is lower than that of conventional disks by a factor of 10, and higher than the capacity of memory by a factor of 8.

SSDs bridge the gap between memory-based and disk-based XTP architectures. SSD-based architectures are slightly slower than memory-based systems, but significantly faster than the fastest disk-based systems. The obvious solution is, therefore, to provide a hierarchical storage architecture in XTP systems, where the most volatile data is stored in memory, data accessed less often is stored on SSDs, and conventional disk-based storage is used for long-term persistent data. It also seems reasonable to store memory overflows from memory-based caching on SSDs.

Summary

At this point in time, you should have a basic understanding of the fundamental concepts of integration, and the terminology used with it. You should now understand:

- The basic concepts used in the context of integration architecture
- The different architecture variants, such as point-to-point, hub-and-spoke, pipeline, and SOA
- What service-oriented integration is and why it is important
- The different types of data integration and the accompanying patterns

- The difference between Enterprise Application Integration (EAI) and Enterprise Information Integration (EII)
- The concept of Event Drive Architecture (EDA) and the different types of Event Processing and why they play an important role in integration
- The integration technologies of the future: grid computing and extreme transaction processing (XTP)

In the next chapter, you will learn about the base technologies related to the implementation of solutions based on the Trivadis Integration Architecture Blueprint.

2
Base Technologies

This chapter describes a selection of the base technologies related to the implementation of solutions based on the Trivadis Integration Architecture Blueprint. It will:

- Cover transactions and transaction strategies
- Contain a description of **Open Grid Services infrastructure (OGSi)**, a dynamic, hardware-independent software platform
- Consider **Java Connector Architecture (JCA)**, which is a general architecture for connecting heterogeneous systems
- Explain **Java Business Integration (JBI)** as a standardized description of the functions of an **Enterprise Service Bus (ESB)**
- Describe **Service Component Architecture (SCA)** in terms of a model for developing applications and systems based on a Service-Oriented Architecture (SOA)
- Present **Service Data Objects (SDO)** as a Disconnected Data Architecture
- Cover process modeling, including a description of the most important standards for modeling business processes

The base technologies that currently play a role in the implementation of integration solutions include transactions and standards such as OGSi, JCA, JBI, SCA, and SDO, all of which we will cover in this chapter.

Transactions and transaction strategies have a central function in every type of architecture. Knowledge of the options available, and the differences between the options, is essential when choosing suitable data access strategies. Important aspects include transactional systems, isolation levels, two-phase commit, and global (XA) transactions (a transaction that may span multiple resources, also known as a **Distributed Transaction**).

Open Grid Services infrastructure (OGSi) is a hardware-independent, dynamic software platform which simplifies the process of modularizing distributed applications and their services, and managing them throughout their entire life cycle. The OSGi platform requires a Java Virtual Machine (JVM) and provides a framework on the basis of the JVM. The most important features of OSGi are the OSGi architecture, the component model (the bundles), and the collaborative model.

Java Connector Architecture (JCA) is a general architecture in the Java Enterprise Edition (JEE) environment used to connect heterogeneous systems, such as legacy applications, through a standardized interface in the form of a resource adapter. Other standardized interfaces defined by the JCA specification allow for collaboration with other system components.

The **Java Business Integration (JBI)** specification describes the functionality of a standardized ESB. JBI can also be regarded as a service-oriented meta-container that implements a component architecture. JBI uses two types of containers: service engines and binding components. The service engines contain the business logic, while the binding components merely act as a proxy for the service users.

Service Component Architecture (SCA) is a collection of specifications that describe a model for developing applications and systems on the basis of an SOA. SCA models solutions as groups of service components that provide services and include references to other services. Functionality is made available externally as a service in the form of interfaces. Service components have properties that describe the specific characteristics of the components and are used to configure them.

Service Data Objects (SDO) offer a consistent model for managing data, regardless of its source system and source format. SDO makes use of a Disconnected Data Architecture. Although SCA and SDO can be used independently of one another, a combination of the two specifications represents a powerful and flexible tool for developing distributed applications.

One important base technology used in the majority of integration projects consists of business process modeling tools. The modeling process is always done using graphical tools. The Trivadis Integration Architecture Blueprint envisions the usage of graphical tools that support a clearly defined modeling notation. A number of these notations are available. The most important ones are **Business Process Modeling Notation (BPMN)**, **Event-Driven Process Chain (EPC)**, and **Business Process Execution Language (BPEL)**.

Transactions

Transactions and transaction strategies play a central role in every architecture. A knowledge of the options available and the differences between them is essential when choosing suitable data access strategies. This section covers the aspects relating to integration. These include transactional systems, isolation levels, two-phase commit, and XA transactions.

- **Transactional systems**: These allow for controlled "all-or-nothing" data manipulation.
- **Isolation levels**: These levels coordinate data access by parallel transactions and, depending on the level, determine the visibility of the manipulated data. There are four different isolation levels:
    - serializable
    - repeatable read
    - read committed
    - read uncommitted
- **Two-phase commit**: The two-phase commit is the algorithm on which transactions are based. It requires all the systems participating in a transaction to commit to the successful completion of the transaction.
- **XA transactions**: An XA transaction is a standardized, global transaction that can span several (heterogeneous) resources. XA uses a two-phase commit to ensure that all resources either commit, or rollback, any particular transaction simultaneously.

Transactional systems

Transaction processing systems and the theoretical concepts that lie behind them have existed in one form or another since the 1970s and were developed by database guru Jim Gray (Lindsay 2008).

The purpose of transactions and of the infrastructure components that support them is "all-or-nothing" data manipulation within a unit of work (Gray, Reuter 1993).

The following brief example will help to make this clearer:

Base Technologies

Say you want to make a bank transfer. This involves debiting the amount from your account and crediting it to another account. The bank transfer process, its sub-activities (debiting and crediting), and the data manipulation involved (deducting the amount from the first account, adding it to the second account) represent a unit of work. This takes place within one transaction to ensure that none of the sub-activities are carried out individually, for example, a debit without a credit or vice versa. The two processes are only valid in combination, even if system errors occur. This consistency is made possible by the use of transactions.

All the operations in a transaction are enclosed within a transaction boundary, as shown in the following figure. It contains all the individual operations, which make up the transaction.

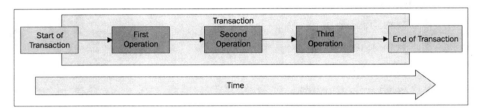

Transactions can be completed in one of two ways:

- Successful — commit
- Unsuccessful — rollback

In the case of a commit, all the changes made during the transaction are reflected in the system. As transactional systems are generally databases or other persistent components, the state changes made in a commit are saved permanently. In the event of a rollback, all the state changes are reversed. Atomic transactions can be nested, but many systems do not support this. In this case, sub-transactions (nested transactions) are provisional, and are only completed when the top-level transaction is completed (commit or abort).

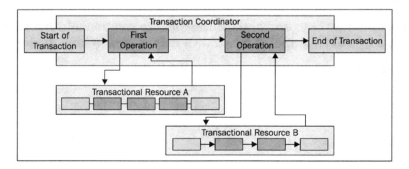

A transaction coordinator is always associated with transactions, as shown in this figure. This infrastructure component manages, monitors, and coordinates the transactions. A coordinator can take the form of an independent component or, for performance reasons, can be part of the application. The coordinator communicates with participants assigned to the transaction (for example, a database and the application which is accessing it) and controls the necessary termination actions, in other words, the commit or the rollback. Different transaction types and mechanisms have different forms of communication and participants (local, remote, distributed, homogeneous, heterogeneous, and so on). The XA protocol for global transactions is often used in distributed environments with several heterogeneous transactional resources (for example, an RDBMS and an XML database).

In many systems, a transaction manager is responsible for managing the transaction coordinators, which coordinate large numbers of transactions. The initiating resource starts the transaction in the transaction manager, and a coordination manager is assigned to the transaction.

Atomic transactions have the following properties, which are also known by the acronym ACID:

- **Atomicity**: The transaction can be successfully completed (commit) or can be unsuccessful as a result of system errors or program crashes (abort). In the first case, all the changes to the data are implemented as if the changes had taken place in one single (atomic) step. In the event of an abort, all the changes made up to this point in the transaction are reversed (rollback), and the system is returned to its status before the transaction started. Atomic transactions cannot be broken down. If an abort occurs, the system is unchanged. Otherwise, all the changes (not just part of them) are implemented.
- **Consistency**: Transactions produce consistent results. As a result, they guarantee that the application and the business logic have a well-defined status.
- **Isolation**: When concurrent transactions are processed, the interim results that occur during the transaction are not visible to other transactions, as long as this transaction is not yet completed. If several transactions are executed simultaneously, they must not influence each other.
- **Durability**: The system status created by a successful transaction completion (commit) is guaranteed to be durable.

Isolation levels

There are four different transaction isolation levels, or, in other words, states that are recognized separately by different parallel transactions. A partial breakup of strict isolation is permitted in many scenarios to improve performance. In order to provide the highest level of process isolation (serializable), data must be blocked. The process that initiates the transaction puts locks on the data. The result is a reduction in the possible process concurrency, in other words, the possible parallelization. Transactions represent a processing bottleneck. The aim of the additional, more relaxed isolation levels is to improve performance compared to strict serialization, by making optimistic assumptions.

In descending order of isolation properties, that is, with increasing visibility and the related possibility of data inconsistencies, the four isolation levels of the ANSI/ISO SQL standard are:

- Serializable
- Repeatable read
- Read committed
- Read uncommitted

Serializable

All the transactions are completely isolated from each other. They appear to take place serially, one after another. So-called **phantom reads**, which will be explained later in the chapter, cannot occur, as shown in the following diagram:

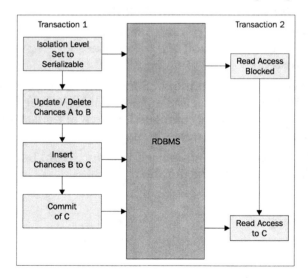

Repeatable read

Data that has been read (in an RDBMS with a SELECT, for example) cannot be changed. On this isolation level, read locks are required on all data that has been read. However, range locks are not needed, as shown in the following diagram:

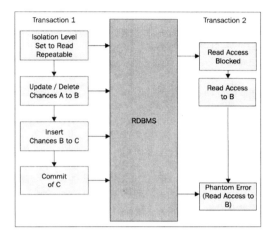

Read committed

Data that has been read (for example with a SELECT) can be changed by other transactions in the background. Read locks are released immediately after the read process has been completed. In contrast, write locks are only released at the end of the transaction, as shown in the following diagram:

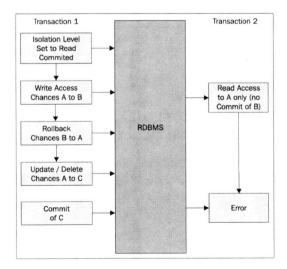

Read uncommitted

On this isolation level, so-called **dirty reads** are possible. Data in **transaction 1** is visible to **transaction 2**, although **transaction 1** has not yet been successfully completed (committed).

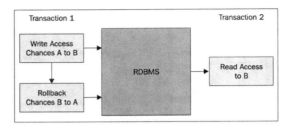

Phantom reads

A phantom read occurs when **transaction 2** can read data created by **transaction 1**, but **transaction 1** has not yet been completed with a commit. Phantom reads can take place in the following ANSI/ISO SQL standard isolation levels:

- Repeatable read
- Read committed
- Read uncommitted

Phantom reads are not possible in the serializable isolation level. The following table gives an overview of this:

Isolation level	Behavior		
	Dirty read	Non-repeatable read	Phantom read
Serializable	No	No	No
Repeatable Read	No	No	Yes
Read Committed	No	Yes	Yes
Read Uncommitted	Yes	Yes	Yes

Different products use the possible isolation levels and the standardized versions in very different ways. In many cases, only a subset of the four options is supported. In some products, additional product-specific syntax must be added to a `SELECT` to enforce a read lock.

Two-Phase Commit protocol (2PC)

The Two-Phase Commit is the basic mechanism for implementing global transactions. The Two-Phase Commit protocol is a distributed algorithm, which requires all the resources in a distributed system that are participating in a transaction to complete the transaction successfully (commit). The result is that all the resources complete the transaction with a *commit*, or reverse it with an *abort*. This is also guaranteed in the event of network errors and/or server failures. A server node takes on the role of coordinator. On each of the participating nodes, there must be the possibility of buffering the local transaction status in order to ensure that, if a server crashes, the transaction can be canceled and the log data is never lost or corrupted (except, of course, in the case of total failures). In addition, the participating nodes must be able to communicate with one another. In particular, where there is a heavy transaction load, the communication latency of the network can be a significant performance factor.

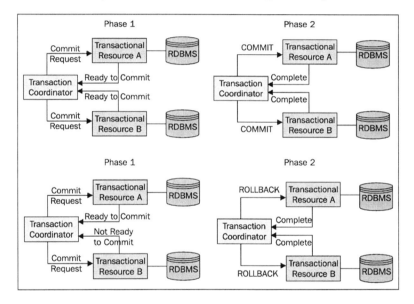

The concept of Two-Phase Commit is the result of implementing the algorithm, which can be divided into the commit request and the commit phases, as shown in this diagram.

- **Commit request**: The transaction coordinator asks the participating resources if they are prepared to commit. Depending on the local transaction results (commit or abort), the individual resources send a corresponding reply.
- **Commit**: On the basis of the result of the commit request phase, the transaction coordinator instructs the participating resources to implement a commit or abort locally.

Base Technologies

This protocol is shown in the following diagram:

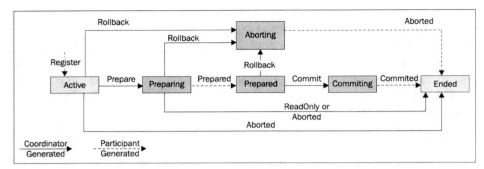

It is initiated by the transaction coordinator when the final step in the transaction is reached. A Two-Phase Commit is made possible by the bidirectional communication of the XA protocol. The Two-Phase Commit is not possible in non-XA transactions, as these protocols are unidirectional and the transaction manager cannot receive any responses from the resource manager. The majority of transaction managers communicate with the resource managers in phase 1 and 2 in parallel in multiple threads, in order to improve performance. By parallelizing communication, the resources can be released at the earliest possible point.

XA transactions

An XA transaction is a global (top-level) transaction, which can span several (heterogeneous) resources, as shown in the next diagram. A non-XA transaction only ever involves a single resource.

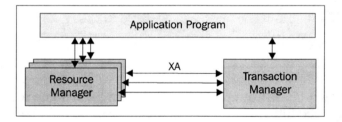

The **X/Open XA** specification describes a bidirectional interface at system level for a communication bridge between several local resource managers on the one hand, and a global transaction manager on the other (OpenGroup 1991). The transaction manager controls the transaction, manages the lifecycle of the transaction, and coordinates one or more resources. The resource manager is responsible for controlling and managing its assigned resource (for example, a database or a message queue).

Because of its bi-directionality, XA uses the Two-Phase Commit protocol. In comparison with atomic transactions, XA has a certain coordination overhead, which can have a negative impact on performance. For this reason, XA should only be chosen when multiple resources are being used simultaneously (in the same transaction context).

> XA is only needed if different resources (for example, two databases, not two tables) are accessed in the same transaction. This includes those scenarios where really only one single transaction is needed. As a result, read-only accesses that need no locks can be implemented without XA. (See also the information about transaction isolation levels.) However, XA supports read-only scenarios of this kind by means of optimizations and, therefore, in these cases the use of XA does not normally result in reductions in performance.

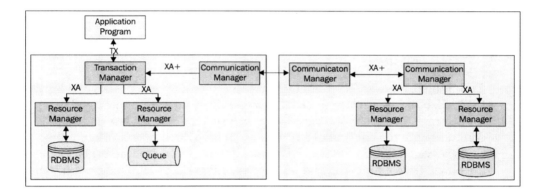

The most common scenario in which XA is used is the simultaneous update of a relational database and a message queue (or message topic) in one transaction, as shown in the preceding image. Other prevalent scenarios of this kind include accesses to two or more databases, or several messaging systems (Rahm 1994).

An XA transaction must coordinate all the participating resource types in the event of a rollback, and must isolate the updates from other transactions (see the information on transaction isolation). Without XA, messages that are sent to a queue or a topic may be read before the transaction is completed. If XA is used, the queue (or the topic) is only released when the transaction has been successfully completed, which means that other transactions do not have access to the message.

OSGi

OSGi is a hardware-independent, dynamic software platform that simplifies the process of modularizing distributed applications and their services, and managing them throughout their entire life cycle (Wütherich et al. 2008). The OSGi platform requires a Java Virtual Machine (JVM) and provides a framework on the basis of the JVM. The OSGi alliance (Open Service Gateway initiative) is an industry consortium consisting of a number of manufacturers from different sectors, which originally developed the platform for use in embedded systems. The most important features of OSGi are as follows:

- **OSGi architecture**: OSGi defines the following layers as its base architecture:
    - Execution environment
    - Module
    - Life cycle
    - Services
    - Security
    - Applications
- **Component model**: The fundamental component model consists of a **bundle**. In OSGi, bundles are also referred to as **services**, which are managed in a service registry. However, the concept of a service in OSGi has nothing in common with the concept of a service in an SOA. The specification of the OSGi service platform defines a runtime environment (container) based on a Java Virtual Machine and Java base architecture. OSGi focuses on the component, which is packaged as a bundle, and which can publish its interface through the service registry, making it available for use. A monitored life cycle is defined for such components.
- **Collaborative Software Environment**: OSGi bundles can collaborate through the OSGi service registry, in which the services a bundle provides are registered.

The specification of the OSGi service platform defines a runtime environment (container) based on a Java Virtual Machine (JVM). One of the important enhancements is the option of equipping the software bundles with independent class loaders and, therefore, running different versions of the same software in parallel on the same JVM. In addition, the OSGi container gives the bundles their own service life cycle, which enables services to be installed, started, stopped, removed, and updated at runtime. Both these factors—versioning and life cycle—are of particular interest in productive environments where high levels of availability are needed. OSGi is therefore ideal for integrating embedded systems, for example, as there is no maintenance window needed for upgrading components.

OSGi has published 4 specifications. The majority of OSGi implementations are based on the release 3 specification from 2003 (OGSi 2003). Well-known implementations include the Eclipse 3.0 platform (Gruber et al. 2005) and the "software in the car" platform developed by BMW (Saad 2003) and Daimler (Heinisch, Simons 2004). As of October 2009, there are five certified OSGi implementations for release 4.

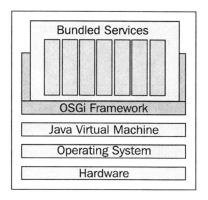

The architecture of the OSGi service platform enables a range of independent service modules to be run in parallel on the same JVM and allows them to be monitored, managed, and updated throughout the entire software life cycle, as shown in the preceding diagram. Remote maintenance is also possible. The interdependencies of bundles are resolved and managed by the OSGi container. The implementations and products that are currently available consist of the OSGi framework and a number of existing software bundles, which, because of their modular structure, can be dynamically added to or removed from a runtime environment.

The current OSGi specification focuses on the component, which is packaged as a bundle. A compoment can publish its interface using the service registry and make it available for use. Components of this kind have a monitored life cycle with options for (re)deployment.

The OSGi framework covers the following points:

- Applications can share one individual virtual machine
- Class loader problems
- The isolation and security of individual applications and services
- Controlled communication and collaboration between applications
- The use of shared resources (such as libraries)

- Life cycle management of applications and services (for example, versioning applications and services)
- Policies are offered by bundles

OSGi architecture

The most important layers of the OSGi architecture are the execution environment, modules, life cycle management, and service registry, as shown in the following diagram:

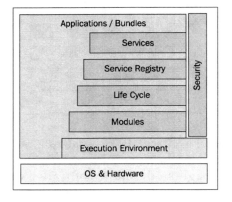

Let's have a look at these layers one by one:

- **Execution environment**: A Java environment, such as J2SE.
- **Modules**: All the classes and resources grouped together as bundles. A bundle can include entire applications, parts of applications, individual service components, and entire libraries. The starting point at runtime is the OSGi system bundle, which makes the OSGi software infrastructure available.
- **Life cycle management**: A defined life cycle for each bundle in the form of an API. This API has the following life cycle statuses, as shown in the following diagram:
    - install
    - resolve
    - start
    - stop
    - refresh
    - update
    - uninstall

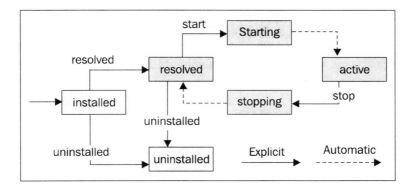

- **Service registry**: The management of all services. This includes identifying services on the basis of their interface definition or properties, and sending notifications between services. It also involves binding to one or more services using program controls, pre-defined standard behavior rules, and distribution configurations.

OSGi bundles

The OSGi component model consists of bundles. These are services, which are managed in a service registry. However, the OSGi service is nothing more than the general interface concept of a software component. It defines a decoupled component model that supports the reusability and the use of small components.

A bundle represents an application deliverable, which is similar to an application executable, in the form of a JAR file. A bundle registers one or more services. A service is specified in a Java interface and can be implemented by several bundles. Services are bound to the bundle life cycle. A query language can be used to search for services registered by other bundles.

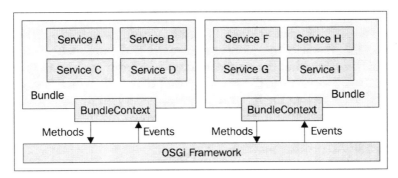

A bundle contains program code, additional resources (optional), and a manifest file that defines the bundle context. The OSGi framework reads the manifest and installs the code and resources in the OSGi runtime environment on this basis. Dependencies with other bundles and services are also resolved using the information in the manifest. At runtime, the framework starts the bundle via the bundle activator and manages the class path and the dependencies (references to other bundles and services). The framework can also stop a bundle by means of the bundle activator.

Collaborative model

Bundles can collaborate in two ways:

- Through service objects
- As shared bundles/packages (package sharing)

A dynamic registry allows a bundle to find other service objects. The framework manages the dependencies between the bundles and services transparently.

Java Connector Architecture (JCA)

JCA is a general architecture in the Java Enterprise Edition (JEE) environment used to connect heterogeneous systems, such as legacy applications, using a standardized interface in the form of a resource adapter. Agreements (contracts) laid down in the JCA specification guarantee collaboration with other system components (JCASpec 2003).

Uses

Java Connector Architecture (JCA) defines standards for connecting the Java Enterprise Edition platform with heterogeneous, distributed **Enterprise Information Systems (EIS)**. JCA enables EIS to be integrated with application servers and business applications as a result of its developer API and manufacturer API specifications. This guarantees that resource adapters are reusable. The manufacturer of a business application can be certain that the application will communicate in a uniform way with a different EIS. In the same way, the manufacturer of an EIS, which is supplied with a JCA adapter can be sure that the EIS can be addressed by all the applications on a Java EE application server, and that the EIS can be integrated into a Java EE architecture in compliance with Java standards. JCA adapters can also be used to integrate an EIS into an ESB or into a BPEL process server.

JCA supports the request/response model with transactions that are more or less short-lived, for example, those from a database environment. JCA does not support more complex, long-lasting transactions, such as those required in workflows and integration scenarios. Java Business Integration (JBI), covered later, which has a communication concept based on the mediated message exchange pattern, is intended to close this gap in the Java EE standard.

JCA components

Each of the components of JCA are detailed in the following figure:

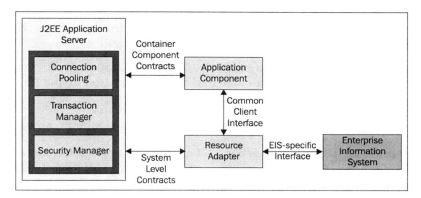

Let's take a look at these components one by one:

- **Resource adapter**: This is the core of the JCA functionality and contains the Java interfaces/classes in the form of the resource adapter archive. The resource adapter runs in an application server.
- **Common Client Interface (CCI)**: The CCI is the API for the resource adapter. It is used to implement the application contract. This is the API applications use to access the EIS.
- **Container-Component Contracts**: These link the application that uses a JCA adapter and the application server. They define the services provided by the component.
- **System-Level Contracts**: These link the application server and the EIS. They also extend the application server with regard to the EIS, so that connection pooling, transaction management, and security management can be used when accessing an EIS. They add connection pooling, transaction management, and security management functionality to the application server.
- **Enterprise Information System**: This is the system with which the connection is to be created using JCA.

Contracts

JCA defines a series of different system-level contracts (agreements), which determine the way in which the application server, JCA, EIS, and application work together:

- **Connection management**: This concerns managing the connection pool with the EIS. The application is provided with connections from this pool, and the application server is responsible for making valid connections available. The functionality for putting in place and testing the connection to the EIS must be in place.
- **Transaction management**: This allows the application server to use a transaction manager to support transactions across several resource managers. The contract also enables internal EIS transaction mechanisms to be used without the need for an external transaction manager.
- **Security management**: This supports a secure environment on the application server in order to protect valuable information provided by the EIS.

Optional system contracts are available covering life cycle management, work management, transaction inflow, and message inflow management, as detailed next:

- **Life cycle management**: This contract enables the application server to manage the life cycle of the resource adapter. It provides a mechanism for the application server to bootstrap a resource adapter during application server startup, or during the installation of the adapter. It also provides a means for the application server to notify the resource adapter instance when it is uninstalled, or when an orderly shutdown of the application server takes place.
- **Work management**: This contract ensures that the application manager is responsible for thread management and the thread pool. Resource adapters can transfer their activities (monitoring network end points, calling application components, and so on) as individual instances to the application server for execution. The adapter is no longer responsible for managing threads itself. Instead, the application server must create new threads for execution or take them from a pre-configured pool. However, the resource adapter continues to control the transaction context where the threads are executed under the control of the application server.
- **Transaction inflow management**: This contract enables the resource adapter to propagate a transaction imported from the EIS to the application server. It also ensures that the resource adapter transfers calls for transaction completion initiated by the EIS, or calls for crash recovery, to the application server to guarantee that the ACID properties of the transaction behavior are not lost.

- **Message inflow management**: This contract allows the resource adapter to provide asynchronous delivery of messages to the message end points of the application server, regardless of the specific message style, semantics, and infrastructure. The contract also describes an option for expanding the application server in order to integrate different message providers [Java Messaging Service (JMS), Java API for XML Messaging (JAXM)] using the concept of a resource adapter.

Java Business Integration (JBI)

The functionality of an ESB is described in general terms in the **Java Business Integration (JBI)** specification (Ten-Hove, Walker 2005). JBI implements a component architecture. JBI is based primarily on two constructs: service engines and binding components. The service engines contain the business logic, while the binding components merely act as a proxy for the service users (Wallrab 2005).

The tasks of a JBI component are as follows:

- Receiving and sending messages. In JBI this is carried out by the binding components.
- Providing interfaces for format conversions. The converter and the business logic needed to transform messages are referred to as the service engine in JBI.
- Installing components (binding component or service engine).
- Deploying components (binding component or service engine).
- Providing mechanisms for managing the life cycle of a component.
- Controlling and monitoring components.

Requests from one component to another are decoupled, and take the form of messages, which the JBI infrastructure passes to the recipients. JBI supports different message exchange patterns:

- **One-way**: The service consumer issues a request to the service provider. No path for reporting error messages is provided.
- **Reliable one-way**: Similar to the one-way pattern, but the provider can inform the consumer of a fault through a response path.
- **Request/response**: The service consumer issues a request to the service provider and waits for a response. In this case, the provider can also inform the consumer of a fault.
- **Request/optional response**: The service consumer issues a request to the service provider. A response is optional. Both the consumer and the provider can inform each other of faults.

Base Technologies

JBI components

The most important JBI components are detailed in the following diagram:

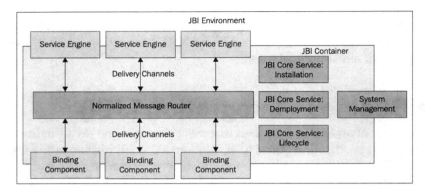

Let's take a look at these components one by one:

- **JBI environment**: A JBI environment is represented by an individual Java Virtual Machine. Therefore, JBI can take the form of an independent ESB, or can be integrated into an application server and its JVM. Where the environment is integrated into an application server, the **Enterprise JavaBean (EJB)** components installed on the server can function as service providers, or as consumers of the ESB.

- **JBI container**: This is comparable to the EJB container of a Java EE application server. The JBI environment itself is a container, which provides service engines and binding components.

- **Pluggable components**: Service engines (SEs) and binding components (BCs) are pluggable components. They are connected to the normalized message router through delivery channels, which allows them to communicate with one another.

- **Service engine (SE)**: These are service providers or consumers that are installed locally in a JBI environment. They represent the business components or the essential functionality that supports the business logic, such as **Extensible Stylesheet Language** (XSL) transformations or database accesses.

- **Binding components (BCs)**: These encapsulate the communications and decouple the communication functionality from the business components (SEs). Binding components allow remote access to distributed services, and also enable distributed services to access the JBI environment.

- **Normalized Message Router (NMR)**: This is the backbone of the JBI architecture. All communications between providers and consumers pass through this router. The NMR uses a canonical format.

- **Normalized message**: This type of message has two parts. There is the header, which contains the metadata (metadata in this context is also referred to as **message context data**), and the payload, in the form of an XML structure that contains the normalized message. The structure of the normalized message is comparable to that of XML messages from **Java Message Service (JMS)**.
- **Delivery channel (DC)**: This connects a message source with a message target. A channel is a virtual construct that conceals the communication details from the providers and consumers and decouples them from the NMR. Delivery channels connect components (providers and consumers) to the NMR, which is responsible for coordinating communications. Channels are logical addresses in the ESB that encapsulate the physical addresses.

Service Component Architecture (SCA)

Service Component Architecture (SCA) is a collection of OASIS (a non-profit consortium driving the adoption of open standards for the global information society) specifications, which describe a model for developing applications and systems on the basis of an SOA (Edwards 2007). SCA models solutions as groups of service components that provide services and include references to other services. Functionality is made available externally as a service in the form of interfaces. Service components have properties that describe the specific characteristics of the components, and are used to configure them.

Services can be combined to form composites. A composite is a composition of SCA components that belong together. These components represent a coarse granular business function and form a separate, functional, reusable unit. Composite services can also contain components that are only used within these composites. The functionality of these internal components is not, however, made available externally as a service in the form of interfaces.

Bindings describe how a service can be accessed. SCA has declarative mechanisms for this purpose, which are based on open specifications. The specifications not only determine how the defined bindings that are currently available can be described, but also how extensions for new protocols should be implemented.

SCA specification

The SCA specification is made up of four parts, as detailed in the following diagram:

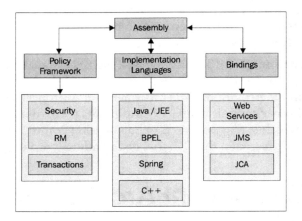

Let's discuss these four parts further:

- **SCA assembly model**: This describes how SOA applications are created with SCA. It also defines how individual modules, in the form of components, can be combined and integrated to produce more complex modules, and how these modules communicate.
- **SCA policy framework**: This defines how security, transaction behavior, message exchange, and reliable messaging can be specified declaratively for a service.
- **SCA client and implementation**: This defines how SCA components can be implemented in different programming languages and on different platforms (for example Java, .NET, C++).
- **SCA binding specification**: This describes how various access technologies and protocols (such as SOAP, JMS, RMI-IIOP, REST, HTTP) can be used.

SCA elements

SCA and SCA components include the elements detailed in the following diagram:

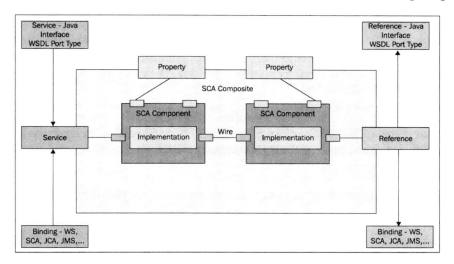

Here's a brief description of these elements:

- **Service**: A service represents the starting point for access to an SCA component or composite.
- **Reference**: A reference is a pointer to an external service.
- **Binding**: This is both an interface and a binding. In this case, an interface is an external declaration of the service, represented by a Java interface, a **Web Service Definition Language (WSDL)** port type, a **Business Process Execution Language (BPEL)** partner link, a C++ class, and so on. An interface binding can be bound to a service or a reference.
- **Property**: This is a type/value pair used to describe and configure specific characteristics of the component.
- **Implementation**: This defines the way in which an SCA component is implemented or, in other words, the form that the logic takes. The implementation types can be some Java code, for example, but can also be a human interaction.
- **Wire**: This is the mechanism that links two SCA components together. Normally, one component's reference is bound to the service offered by another component.

Composites

A composite component is a logical construct that consists of SCA components that can form part of a single process on a single computer, or can be distributed across several processes on several computers. An application can be created with a single composite. The individual SCA components that make up the composite can be implemented using the same or different technologies. SCA applications can be called by a non-SCA technology, such as a web service client or a **servlet**. They can also access external data sources and other applications.

An SCA composite is described by a configuration file. This uses an XML format, **Service Component Definition Language (SCDL, or Skiddle)**, to describe the components and the details of their relationships with one another, and with other external components.

Composites and components are the core elements of every SCA application.

Service Data Objects (SDO)

Service Data Objects (SDO) offer a consistent model for managing data, regardless of its source system and source format (Beatty et al. 2003). SDO makes use of a Disconnected Data Architecture. SDO supports the management of data that has been decoupled from its source and transported across different systems and tiers, by subsequently synchronizing it with its source again. SCA and SDO can be used independently of one another, and their specifications have nothing in common. However, a combination of the two specifications represents a powerful and flexible tool for developing distributed applications.

The SDO specification was published jointly by BEA and IBM, standardized as **JSR 235,** and transferred to the **Open Service-Oriented Architecture (OSOA).** The current version of the specification is version 2.1 for Java, COBOL, C++, and C (Barber, Edwards 2007).

SDO architecture

SDO consists of data objects, data graphs, and data access services, as shown in the following diagram:

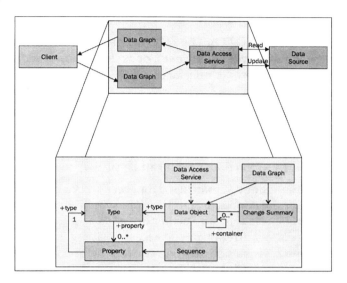

Now let's take a look at these three components:

- **Data object**: This is the object-oriented representation of the fundamental data. It encapsulates the data attributes in the form of simple values, as a reference to other objects and the descriptive metadata.
- **Data graph**: This represents a **Data Transfer Object** (DTO), which is transferred between the different tiers of an architecture. It can be made up of several individual data objects by using object graphs. These can include, for example, a master data set consisting of several detail data sets and their relationships to one another. In addition to the user data, changes to the object are included, or in other words, all the data objects that have been added, modified, and deleted are included.
- **Data access service**: This is the interface between the client and the data sources. The data access service is responsible for decoupling the applications from the physical accesses to the source systems, which hold the data. This service uses the data access object pattern.

SDO also provides metadata for describing data objects, including data types, relationships between data objects, and constraints. The metadata API is used by tools and other frameworks to simplify the development of applications that make use of SDO.

Implemented patterns

SDO implements a series of patterns, including:

- **Data Access Object (DAO)**: The DAO encapsulates the calls to the data access layer.
- **Data Transfer Object (DTO)**: The DTO is a transport container for data objects moving between different layers, tiers, or systems, and it reduces the number of method calls from remote interfaces.
- **Entity object (EO)**: The EO is an object from the application domain. It represents entities from the business domain.
- **Disconnected data usage**: Data objects can be generated by data system accesses. The connection to the data system can be broken and recreated later, and changes to the data object can be propagated to the data system.
- **Optimistic concurrency semantics data access**: As a result of disconnected data usage, after the connection to the data system has been broken, the resources must be released for further accesses as part of the resource management process. An optimistic access strategy is put in place in order to maintain data consistency, despite competing accesses. When changes to data are propagated back to the data system once the connection has been re-established, the data in question is checked to determine whether it has been modified by another process in the meantime (after the initial query). This involves, for example, comparing the time stamps or counters. The original data set (the data that was read initially) may also be included with the modified data, and compared with the current data in the data system.

Process modeling

One important base technology used in the majority of integration projects consists of business process modeling tools. The modeling process is always done using graphical tools. The Trivadis Integration Architecture Blueprint envisages the usage of graphical tools that support a clearly defined modeling notation. A number of these notations are available. The most important are **Event-Driven Process Chain (EPC)**, **Business Process Modeling Notation (BPMN)**, and **Business Process Execution Language (BPEL)**, which are all explained next:

Event-driven Process Chain (EPC)

The Event-driven Process Chain (EPC) is a model used to represent business processes in an organization, as part of business process modeling (Scheer, Werth 2005). The notation was developed as a part of the **Architecture of Integrated Information Systems (ARIS)** for modeling business processes, and is a central element of the ARIS concept (Scheer et al. 2006). An example of an EPC is shown in the following diagram:

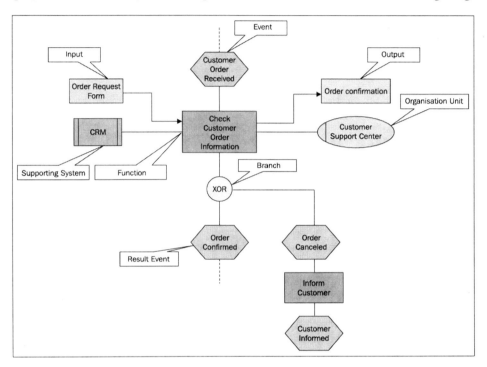

EPCs represent work processes in graphical form using semi-formal modeling language with syntax rules. This allows business processes to be systematized and parallelized, which saves time and money. As decisions are made within the process on the basis of conditions and rules, logical operators are used in the EPC (AND, OR, EXCLUSIVE OR). In addition to these operators, the basic model of the Event-Driven Process Chain includes events and functions. Objects are joined together in directional diagrams with lines and arrows in a 1:1 mapping (with the exception of logical links). In a chain of this kind, events and functions are alternate objects. This means that they form an alternating sequence, which results in a diagram being created. An important feature of the EPC is the representation of the functions that make up a process in a chronological and logical sequence.

Business Process Modeling Notation (BPMN)

The Business Process Modeling Notation (BPMN) is an OMG standard (OMG 2008). It provides symbols that enable technical and IT specialists to model business processes and workflows (White 2004). A BPMN example is shown in the following diagram:

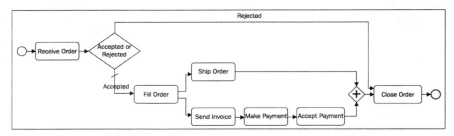

The BPMN is designed to represent business processes in graphical form. The BPMN standards document also defines the semantics, in other words, the meaning of the symbols, but it places less emphasis on this aspect and does not focus on formal definitions. BPMN diagrams are referred to as **Business Process Diagrams (BPD)**, and are intended to provide support for experts who are representing or developing processes. The specification does not include a standardized format for storing and exchanging diagrams that are created using BPMN.

The BPMN standard defines how a BPMN diagram can be converted to BPEL, so that the processes described can be run by a software package. However, BPMN and BPEL are not able to express the same types of concepts.

[It is worth noting that BPMN models are generally underspecified, and lack some of the details required for execution.]

The graphical elements of the BPMN can be broken down into:

- **Flow objects**: These are nodes in the business process diagram. Flow objects represent either an *activity* (a task to be completed), a *gateway* (decision point), or an *event*.
- **Connecting objects**: These are the links in the business process diagram. Connecting objects are either *sequence flows*, which link activities, gateways, and events, or *message flows*, which illustrate the movement of messages between different objects.
- **Swimlanes**: These are the objects used to represent participants and systems.
- **Artifacts**: Other elements such as *data objects* (the artifacts processed by a business process), *groups* (the option of creating groups to represent sub-processes), and *annotations* (comments) are referred to as artifacts.

Business Process Execution Language (BPEL)

The first versions of Business Process Execution Language (BPEL) and BPEL4WS for web services were developed by IBM, Microsoft, Siebel, BEA, SAP, and Oracle in 2002 (version 1.1 was issued in April 2003). XLANG (from Microsoft) and WSFL (from IBM) were integrated into BPEL (Andrews et al. 2003). The most recent version (version 2.0) was published in the form of a committee draft on January 31, 2007 (Alves et al. 2006).

BPEL allows a process to be described and represented. The description takes a graphical form and is created in a BPEL editor. However, other workflow modeling techniques can also be used. In contrast to the other methods, the modeled business process can directly generate the controls for the workflow engine (BPEL engine). BPEL enables various different services to be linked together to form a complete application.

BPEL distinguishes between two different types of business processes: business protocols and executable business processes. **Business protocols** are abstract process descriptions that act as interaction patterns for the **executable business processes**.

A BPEL process consists of a process interface and a process diagram. The process interface is formulated in WSDL, as every BPEL process is a web service. The process diagram defines the process flow (actions), the instancing method (correlation sets), the partners (partner link), and the fault management mechanisms (fault manager).

The process is structured using a combination of hierarchical blocks and diagrams. The blocks can be nested. In BPEL they take the form of structured activities, which are similar to the constructions of a structured programming language. One typical feature is the `<switch>` structured activity, which defines a conditional implementation. Structured activities control the flow of atomic activities and form the nodes of an execution tree. The atomic activities control the individual steps in a BPEL process, for example, `<invoke>` calls a web service.

The application of process modeling

Almost every integration project needs business processes and other workflows to be modeled. A service-oriented integration would be almost impossible without the use of BPEL. Data integrations are usually accompanied by modeling of Extract, Transform, and Load (ETL) processes. In addition, the majority of commercial ESB and middleware infrastructures use graphical tools to model the routing of messages, or have their own process modeling tools. This means that it is advisable for every integration architect to be familiar with the use of these tools. Currently, the most important process modeling notation is BPEL.

Summary

Having read this chapter, you should now have a better understanding of the base technologies related to the implementation of solutions based on the Trivadis Integration Architecture Blueprint. You should now be familiar with:

- Transactions and transaction strategies
- Open Grid Services infrastructure (OGSi) — the dynamic, hardware-independent software platform
- Java Connector Architecture (JCA) — the general architecture for connecting heterogeneous systems in the Java EE world
- Java Business Integration (JBI) — a standardization of the functions of an Enterprise Service Bus (ESB)
- Service Component Architecture (SCA) — a component model for developing applications and systems based on a SOA
- Service Data Objects (SDO) — supporting a Disconnected Data Architecture
- Process modeling and the most important standards for modeling business processes

We have now covered the fundamental concepts and technologies related to the implementation of integration solutions. In the next chapter, you will finally learn what the Trivadis Integration Architecture Blueprint is, how it is structured into different layers, and why it has been defined this way.

3
Integration Architecture Blueprint

This chapter describes the Trivadis Integration Architecture Blueprint and its components. It will:

- Cover the information flow and the mutual dependencies between the components of the blueprint
- Define the communication layer, which is part of the integration domain level
- Contain a description of the collection/distribution layer, which forms part of the integration domain level
- Explain the mediation layer, which belongs to the integration domain level
- Describe the process layer, which is a component of the application level
- Cover notation and visualization, which contains information about tools for integration architects

Dissecting the Trivadis Integration Architecture Blueprint

The **Trivadis Integration Architecture Blueprint** specifies the building blocks needed for the effective implementation of integration solutions. It ensures consistent quality in the implementation of integration strategies as a result of a simple, tried-and-tested structure, and the use of familiar integration patterns (Hohpe, Wolf 2004).

Standards, components, and patterns used

The Trivadis Integration Architecture Blueprint uses common standardized techniques, components, and patterns, and is based on the layered architecture principle.

A **layered architecture** divides the overall architecture into different **layers** with different responsibilities. Depending on the size of the system and the problem involved, each layer can be broken down into further layers. Layers represent a logical construct, and can be distributed across one or more physical tiers. In contrast to **levels**, layers are organized hierarchically, and different layers can be located on the same level. Within the individual layers, the building blocks can be strongly cohesive. Extensive decoupling is needed between the layers. The rule is that higher-level layers can only be dependent on the layers beneath them and not vice versa. Each **building block** in a layer is only dependent on building blocks in the same layer, or the layers beneath. It is essential to create a layer structure that isolates the most important cohesive design aspects from one another, so that the building blocks within the layers are decoupled.

The blueprint is process oriented, and its notation and structure are determined by the blueprint's dependencies and information flow in the integration process. An explanation of how the individual layers, their building blocks, and tasks can be identified from the requirements of the information flow is given on the basis of a simple scenario. In this scenario, the information is transported from one source to another target system using an integration solution.

In the blueprint, the building blocks and scenarios are described using familiar design patterns from different sources:

- (Hohpe, Wolf 2004)
- (Adams et al. 2001)
- (Coral8 2007)
- (Russel et al. 2006)

These patterns are used in a shared context on different layers. The Trivadis Integration Architecture Blueprint includes only the integration-related parts of the overall architecture, and describes the specific view of the **technical integration domain** in an overall architecture. It focuses on the information flow between systems in the context of domain-driven design.

Domain-driven design is a means of communication, which is based on a profound understanding of the relevant business domain. This is subsequently modeled specifically for the application in question. Domain models contain no technical considerations and are restricted exclusively to business aspects. Domain models represent an abstraction of a business domain, which aims to capture the exemplary aspects of a specific implementation for this domain. The objectives are:

- To significantly simplify communication between domain experts and developers by using a common language (the domain model)
- To enable the requirements placed on the software to be defined more accurately and in a more targeted way
- It must be possible to describe, specify, and document the software more precisely and more comprehensibly, using a clearly defined language, which will make it easier to maintain

The technical aspects of architecture can be grouped into domains in order to create specific views of the overall system. These domains cover security, performance, and other areas. The integration of systems and information also represents a specific view of the overall system, and can be turned into a domain.

Integration domain is used to mean different things in different contexts. One widely used meaning is "application domain," in other words, a clearly defined, everyday problem area where computer systems and software are used. Enterprise architectures are often divided into business and technical domains:

- **Business domains** may include training, resource management, purchasing, sales or marketing, for example.
- **Technical domains** are generally areas such as applications, integration, network, security, platforms, systems, data, and information management.

The blueprint, however, sees integration as a technical domain, which supports business domains, and has its own views that can be regarded as complementary to the views of other architecture descriptions.

In accordance with Evans (Evans, 2004), the Trivadis Integration Architecture Blueprint is a *ubiquitous language* for describing integration systems. This and the structure of the integration domain on which it is based, have been tried and tested in a variety of integration projects using different technologies and products. The blueprint has demonstrated that it offers an easy-to-use method for structuring and documenting implementation solutions. As domain models for integration can be formulated differently depending on the target platform (for example, an object-oriented system or a classic ETL solution), the domain model is not described in terms of object orientation. Instead, the necessary functionality takes the form of building blocks (which are often identical with familiar design patterns) on a higher level of abstraction. This makes it possible to use the blueprint in a heterogeneous development environment with profitable results.

An **architecture blueprint** is based on widely used, tried-and-tested techniques, components, and patterns, which are grouped into a suitable structure to meet the requirements of the target domain.

The concepts, the functionality, and the building blocks to be implemented are described in an abstract form in blueprints. These are then replaced or fine-tuned by product-specific building blocks in the implementation project. Therefore, the Trivadis Integration Architecture Blueprint has been deliberately designed to be independent of individual vendors, products, and technologies. It includes integration scenarios and proposals that apply to specific problems, and can be used as aids during the project implementation process. The standardized view of the integration domain and the standardized means of representation enable strategies, concepts, solutions, and products to be compared with one another more easily in evaluations of architectures.

The specifications of the blueprint act as guidelines. Differences between this model and reality may well occur when the blueprint is implemented in a specific project. Individual building blocks and the relationships between them may not be needed, or may be grouped together. For example, the **adapter** and **mapper** building blocks may be joined together to form one component in implementation processes or products.

Structuring the integration blueprint

The following diagram is an overview of the Trivadis Integration Architecture Blueprint. It makes a distinction between the **application and information view** and the **integration view**.

Chapter 3

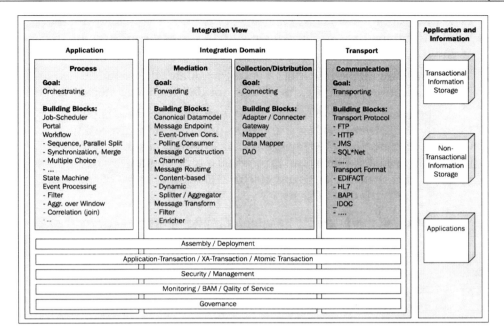

The **application and information view** consists of external systems, which are to be connected together by an integration solution. These are source or target entities in the information flow of an integration solution. Generally one physical system can also take on both roles. The building blocks belonging to the view, and the view itself, must be regarded as external to the integration system that is being described and, therefore, not the subject of the integration blueprint. The external systems can be divided into three main categories:

- **Transactional information storage**: This includes classic relational database management systems (RDBMS) and messaging systems (queues, topics). The focus is on data integration.

- **Non-transactional information storage**: This is primarily file-based systems and non-relational data stores (NoSQL) with a focus on data integration.

- **Applications**: Applications include transactional or non-transactional systems that are being integrated (ERP—Enterprise Resource Planning, CMS—Content Management System, and so on) and can be accessed through a standardized API (web service, RMI/IIOP, DCOM, and so on). The focus is on application and process integration.

The integration view lies at the heart of the integration blueprint and is divided (on the basis of the principle of **divide and conquer**) into the following levels:

- **Transport level**: The transport level encapsulates the technical details of communication protocols and formats for the external systems. It contains:
    - **Communication layer**: The communication layer is part of the transport level, and is responsible for transporting information. This layer links the integration solution with external systems, and represents a type of gateway to the infrastructure at an architectural level. It consists of transport protocols and formats.

- **Integration domain level**: The integration domain level covers the classic areas of integration, including typical elements of the integration domain, such as adapters, routers, and filters. It is divided into:
    - **Collection/distribution layer**: This layer is responsible for connecting components. It is completely separate from the main part of the integration domain (mediation). The building blocks in this layer connect the mediation layer above with the communication layer below. The layer is responsible for encapsulating external protocols and their technical details from the integration application, and transforming external technical formats into familiar internal technical formats.
    - **Mediation layer**: This layer is responsible for forwarding information. Its main task is to ensure the reliable forwarding of information to business components in the process layer, or directly to output channels that are assigned to the collection/distribution layer, and that distribute data to the target systems. This is the most important functionality of the integration domain. In more complex scenarios, the information forwarding process can be enhanced by information transformation, filtering, and so on.

- **Application level**: The application level encapsulates the integration management and process logic. It is an optional level and contains:
    - **Process layer**: The process layer is part of the application level, and is responsible for orchestrating component and service calls. It manages the integration processes by controlling the building blocks in the mediation layer (if they cannot act autonomously).

The integration view contains additional functionality that cannot be assigned to any of the levels and layers referred to above. This functionality consists of so-called cross-cutting concerns that can be used by building blocks from several other layers. Cross-cutting concerns include:

- **Assembly/deployment**: Contains configurations (often declarative or scripted) of the components and services. For example, this is where the versioning of Open Service Gateway initiative (OSGi) services is specified.
- **Transaction**: Provides the transaction infrastructure used by the building blocks in the integration domain.
- **Security/management**: This is the security and management infrastructure used by the building blocks in the integration domain. It includes, for example, libraries with security functionality, JMX agents, and similar entities.
- **Monitoring, BAM, QoS**: These components are used for monitoring operations. This includes ensuring compliance with the defined **Service Level Agreements (SLA)** and **Quality of Service (QoS)**. **Business Activity Monitoring (BAM)** products can be used for monitoring purposes.
- **Governance**: These components and artifacts form the basis for SLAs and QoS. The artifacts include business regulations, for example. In addition, this is where responsibilities, functional and non-functional requirements, and accounting rules for the services/capacities used are defined.

The road to the integration blueprint

The Trivadis Integration Architecture Blueprint connects applications and systems together with its levels and layers. From an integration perspective, the application/system is responsible for providing and storing information (application and information view). The tasks of the integration solution include transporting information from the source systems, together with collecting, transforming, filtering, forwarding, and distributing information, and transporting it to the target systems. These tasks can only be performed efficiently if the integration view has a logical structure. It must be possible for the tasks to be distributed across different layers in order to give improved decoupling.

The fundamental tasks are:

- Transporting
- Connecting
- Forwarding

Integration Architecture Blueprint

These tasks result in the creation of **communication, collection, mediation,** and **distribution layers**. Each layer has a specific role to ensure that it covers the responsibilities and related tasks. These roles are that of a transporter, collector, mediator, and distributor. The information flow in an integration solution determines the call sequence for the building blocks. It is advisable to combine the collection and distribution layers to form a single layer, as both of these layers perform their tasks—collecting and distributing data—using the same building blocks. In the architecture blueprint this layer is referred to as the **collection/distribution layer**. The result of introducing this layer is that the source and target systems are on the same level from the perspective of the integration solution. As a consequence, the direction of the information flow changes.

The integration solution consists of the mediation (forwarding), collection/distribution (connecting), and communication (transporting) layers. The mediation layer requires additional building blocks that control the integration process, as it can seldom act independently or passively. The orchestrator manages the information flow, working together with the job scheduler or workflow building blocks.

The integration blueprint is therefore divided into the following four layers:

- Process
- Mediation
- Collection/distribution
- Communication

The allocation of the various layers of the Trivadis Integration Architecture Blueprint to the three levels **application, integration domain,** and **transport** enables an integration solution to be embedded in an overall architecture. From an application perspective, the management of the information flow as a business process is essential, while standardized and reliable communication is important for the technical infrastructure. In contrast to other common approaches to integration, the integration blueprint is the central component of an overall solution. As a result, the integration architecture is always considered, designed, specified, implemented, and operated as part of the design process for applications and systems.

Applications and integration

In simple cases, a single integration process consists of a source system, which reads information from an integration solution and a target system, to which information from the integration solution is written, as shown in the following diagram:

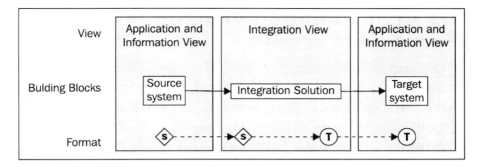

A distinction is made between two different views as follows:

- The application and information view consists of external systems, which are to be connected together using an integration solution. These are source or target entities in the information flow. Generally one physical system can also take on both roles. The external systems can be divided into three main categories: transactional information storage, non-transactional information storage, and applications.
- The integration view lies at the heart of the integration architecture blueprint.

The tasks and the building blocks of the two views are described in the following table:

View	Building block	Task
Application and Information	Source system Target system	Providing information Storing information
Integration	Integration solution	Collecting information from the sources, transporting data using external infrastructure components, transforming and forwarding information, and distributing it to target systems

Source and target systems frequently use different information formats. As a result, the integration solution must be able to process both formats and transform data from one format to another. In the preceding diagram, the information is converted from the **S** (source) into the **T** (target) format, or from the **diamond** to the **circle** format. The more systems and formats that are involved in an integration process, the more comprehensive and complex the transformation logic is. Adaptations to other systems at a later stage are often complicated and costly.

Integration Architecture Blueprint

Layers in the integration solution

The tasks of the integration view include:

- **Transporting information** (communication layer) from the source systems
- **Assembling** information (collection layer)
- **Transforming, filtering,** and **forwarding** (mediation layer)
- **Distributing information** (distribution layer),
- **Transporting information** (communication layer) to the target systems.

This results in the creation of layers, as shown the following diagram:

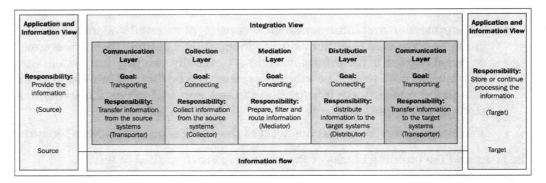

The diagram shows the layers without the optional process layer. In the case of simple information flows, this layer can be omitted. It will be described in a later section.

The division of the integration view into different layers allows for improved decoupling through the **Separation of Concerns (SoC)** and the break down into the following three goals:

- **Transporting**: The communication layer transports the information using the appropriate communication protocols.
- **Connecting**: The collection layer collects the data from the transport building blocks and forwards it to the building blocks of the mediation layer. The distribution layer distributes the data to the transport building blocks and collects it from the mediation layer.
- **Forwarding**: The mediation layer has the goal of forwarding information to the correct building block in the distribution layer. It receives the information from the collection layer.

Each layer has a specific role to ensure that the target systems and the related tasks are covered. The resulting roles are **transporter, collector, mediator,** and **distributor**.

Defining a mediator pattern

A mediator is a software design pattern which belongs to the group of behavioral patterns, because it can influence the running behavior of a program. The pattern is used to manage the cooperative behavior of objects. However, the objects do not cooperate directly with one another, but using a **mediator**.

The mediator provides a standardized interface to replace a series of interfaces belonging to a subsystem.

The use of a mediator brings the following range of benefits:

- The cooperative behavior can be centrally managed.
- Changes in the cooperative behavior can take place independently of the components involved.
- The communication protocol used between the components can be simplified.

Information flow and roles

The addition of roles to the layer diagram enables the identification of the building blocks which achieve the goals and objectives of the integration layers.

The information flow between the source and the target system, the roles of the individual layers, and the formats used are shown in the next diagram:

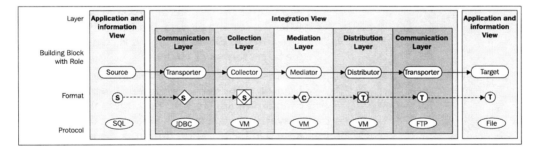

Integration Architecture Blueprint

The following table describes the roles in detail

Layer	Role	Description
Communication	Transporter	Transports the information from the source systems to the **integration solution** or to the adapter building block in the collection layer. The information format is that of the source system. In other words, if a table is accessed, as in this example, through Java Database Connectivity (JDBC) API and SQL, the format is that of an SQL result set.
Collection	Collector	The collector connects the integration solution to the network building block in the communication layer, and can convert the data from the transport format to an internal technical format. In the example, the SQL result set is converted into a Java object.
Mediation	Mediator	The mediator waits actively (**polling**) or passively (**event-driven**) for information and forwards it to one or more potential distributors. The source format can first be transformed into a canonical data format (corresponding to the canonical data model pattern) in order for the forwarding to remain independent of the source system. In the example, before the routing, the data is converted from the source format (**S** diamond) to the canonical format (**C** rhombus). After the routing process, but before the data is forwarded to the distributor, it is converted into the target format (**T** circle).
Distribution	Distributor	The distributor connects the integration solution to the network building block in the communication layer for the target solution. It converts the data from the internal technical format to the transport format. If the target system format is a file, as in the example, the Java object is transformed into a file.
Communication	Transporter	Transports the information from the integration solution to the target systems. In this example, a file is sent using the File Transfer Protocol (FTP).

Information flow and building blocks

The roles of collector, mediator, and distributor describe the tasks involved in a very general form. In practice, it is advisable to break down the roles even further and assign appropriate building blocks to them. The following diagram shows the allocation of different building blocks to the mediation, collection, and distribution layers and their roles:

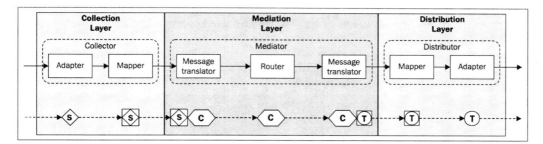

These building blocks are run through one after another, corresponding to the information flow.

The collector role in the collection layer is performed by the following building blocks:

- **Adapter**: connects the collection layer to the building block in the communication layer in order to ensure that there is a connection to the source.
- **Mapper**: converts the data from the transport format to the internal format.

The mediator role in the mediation layer is performed by the following building blocks:

- **Message translator**: converts the internal format into the canonical format on the basis of the canonical data model.
- **Router**: determines the target, in other words, the system that the data will be forwarded to, possibly using the information in the canonical format.
- **Message translator**: converts the canonical format into an internal target format.

The **distributor role** in the **distribution layer** is allocated to the following building blocks:

- **Mapper**: converts the internal source format into the transport format.
- **Adapter**: connects the distribution layer to the building block in the communication layer of the corresponding target system.

Combining the collection and distribution layer

It is advisable to combine the **collection** and **distribution layers** to form a single layer, as both of these layers perform their tasks—collecting and distributing data—using the same building blocks. In the architecture blueprint, this layer is referred to as the **collection/distribution layer**.

This changes the representation of the layers and the information flow, as shown in the following diagram:

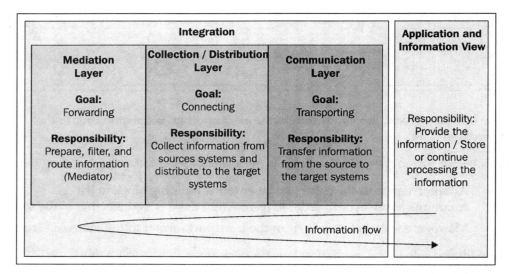

Collection and distribution have been combined to form one layer. There is only one occurrence of the **communication layer** and of the **Application and Information View**. The direction of the information flow also changes. It no longer passes through the layers from left to right. Instead it moves from top right via the mediation layer, and back to bottom right.

Change of direction in the information flow

The representation of the roles in the image below shows the change in the information flow, which now moves from the source system in the top-right corner, through the mediation layer to the target systems in the bottom-right corner.

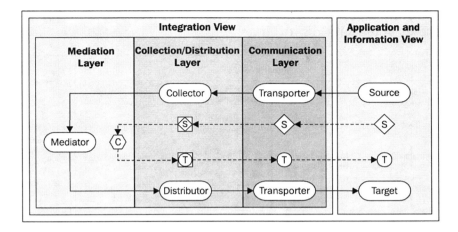

However, the sequence and the functionality of the building blocks and formats remain the same. Only the number of layers and the direction of the information flow change.

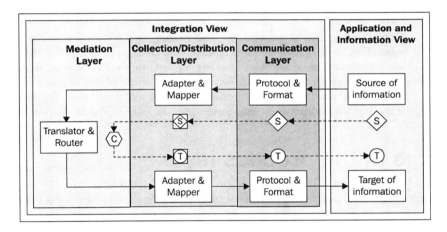

Adding the process layer

The integration solution consists of the mediation (forwarding), collection/distribution (connecting), and communication (transporting) layers. The mediation layer requires additional building blocks that control the integration process, as it can seldom act independently or passively. This is only the case when it is driven by external events or functions as a polling consumer. In all other cases it must be managed, and this role is fulfilled by the **orchestrator** in the process layer.

The most important purpose of the process layer is to orchestrate the information flow, as shown in the following diagram:

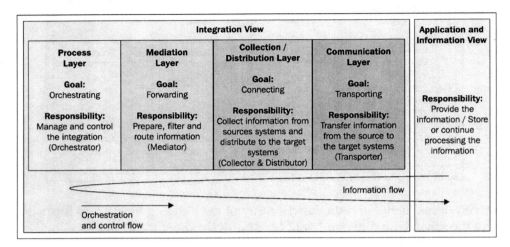

> **Orchestrating**
>
> Orchestrating involves controlling and managing the building blocks in the mediation layer below. In a simple case, this task can be performed by a job-scheduling building block that triggers an integration process. In an SOA environment, BPEL (Business Process Execution Language) can be used to implement entire integration processes which are also allocated to this layer, and which orchestrate building blocks from the mediation layer.

The role of the process layer

Adding the process layer to the information flow, as shown in the following image, results in an additional orchestrator role which must be performed by a specific building block:

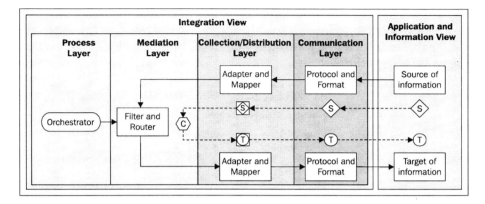

In this case, the orchestrator controls the mediation layer and can therefore start the integration or the information flow, for example. The mediator and the building blocks which implement the mediator functionality become passive entities that are initiated by the process layer.

The building blocks of the process layer

In practice, the role of the orchestrator is, of course, further concretized by using specific building blocks. For example, the tasks of the orchestrator can be carried out by a job-scheduler building block, as shown in this modified diagram:

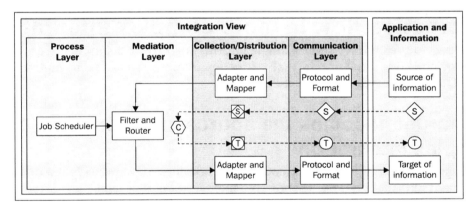

However, the orchestrator in the process layer can also be activated or triggered by a source system, as demonstrated in the following diagram. In this case, the orchestrator role is fulfilled by a workflow or BPEL building block, and by that, implements an integration process.

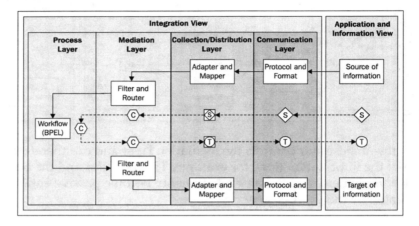

A query or message from an information source initiates the integration process via protocol and format, and through filter and router building blocks. The process is executed autonomously and uses an additional filter and router building block to initiate the target systems.

Information flow in more complex integrations

All the previous examples show a single information flow in a simple integration. However, the layer structure must also function in more complex information flows. The following examples illustrate this.

The target becomes the source in a more complex integration

The target system in the first information flow becomes the source system of the subsequent information flow, as shown in the following diagram:

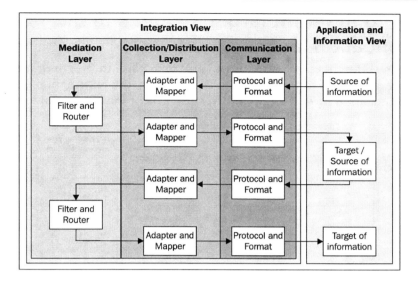

Routing to different target systems in the mediation layer

More complex information flows may have several information target systems. In the example in the following diagram, the information is distributed in the mediation layer using the router building block.

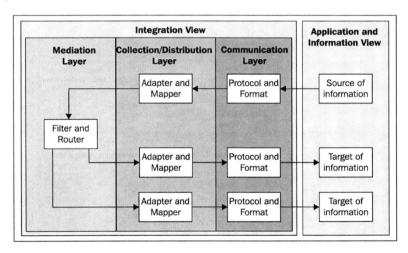

Routing to different target systems in the communication layer

The routing to different target systems can also take place in the communication layer. In the example shown in the following diagram, the information is distributed in the communication layer using publish/subscribe or multicast protocols.

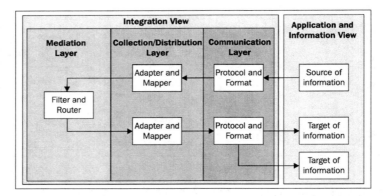

Task sharing in the mediation layer

A layer can share its tasks among several building blocks, which run one after another, as demonstrated in the following diagram. The mediation layer first uses a translator building block to convert the message to a canonical format, then enhances the information using an enrichment building block, and finally forwards the information to the correct target system.

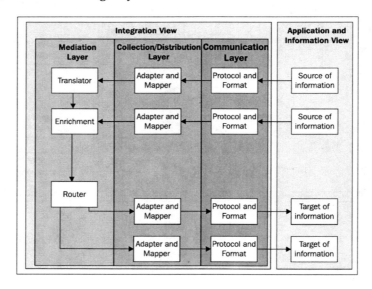

Management using a workflow building block

The process layer can be used to manage more complex integration solutions, by implementing a process-driven integration. One example of the use of a workflow building block is shown in the following diagram:

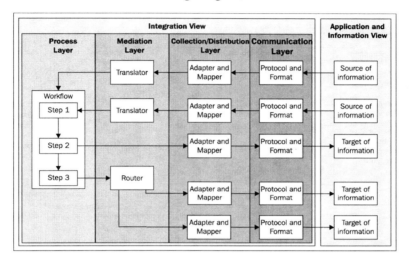

The workflow building block implements an integration process in a flexible way, and is started by a source system. The individual steps in the workflow integrate further systems. In step 1 the information is fetched from one source system, and in step 2 a direct link is established to a target system without using a building block in the mediation layer. Step 3 links in another target system, but in this case the distribution process is delegated to the mediation layer and a router building block.

Allocating layers to levels

A glance at the previous examples shows that the integration process and its implementation take place on three different levels:

- **The communication layer:** This layer encapsulates building blocks made available by the infrastructure.
- **The mediation and collection/distribution layers**: These layers are responsible for integrating two or more systems. They are concerned solely with integration, and the implemented logic can be assigned completely to the integration domain.

- **The process layer:** This layer is optional and is used when an additional external component is needed for managing and controlling the integration process. The implemented logic cannot be assigned exclusively to the integration domain. Application-specific business logic may also be used in implementing business processes.

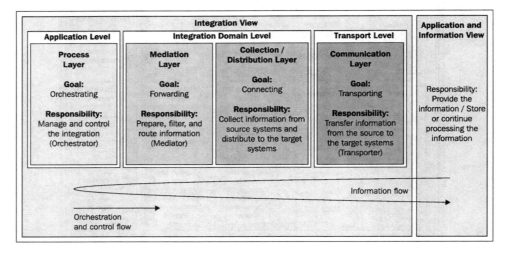

The blueprint allows for this by assigning the four layers shown above to the following three levels:

- **Transport level**: This level contains the building blocks made available by the relevant infrastructure.
- **Integration domain level**: This level contains building blocks that implement the integration.
- **Application level**: This level contains building blocks that implement both integration and application tasks.

This last addition of the levels completes the integration blueprint and leads to the overview diagram, which is repeated here:

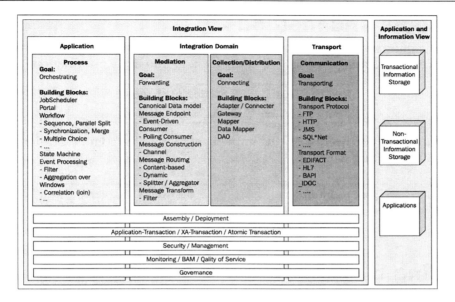

The allocation of the various layers of the Trivadis Integration Architecture Blueprint to the **application**, **integration domain**, and **transport levels**, enables an integration solution to be embedded in an overall architecture. From an application perspective, the management of the information flow as a business process is essential, while standardized and reliable communication is important for the technical infrastructure.

Transport level: Communication layer

The **communication layer** is part of the **transport level** and is responsible for transporting information. This layer links the internal integration solution with external systems. It represents a type of gateway to the infrastructure at an architectural level, and consists of transport protocols and transport formats.

Responsibility

The responsibility of the communication layer is to transport information using standardized protocols and formats.

Concepts and methods

The basic requirements for the implementation of the communication layer are listed in the table below, along with where in the book to find more information.

Requirement	Section of chapter 1
Routing schemes	*Routing schemes*

The base technologies needed for the implementation of the communication layer are listed in the following table.

Base technology	Section of chapter 2
Transactions and their isolation levels and protocols	*Transactions*

Building blocks

Transport protocols and transport formats are the building blocks in the communication layer. The information formats of the external systems (source and target systems) and their interface definitions can be regarded as message formats, which are described in this layer as artifacts. The terms **message protocol** and **message format** have deliberately been generalized, as the blueprint is also intended for use with traditional file-based data transmission processes (for example, in ETL systems). The term "message," which is generally used in the context of message systems, does not seem appropriate here.

Additional information is needed in the implementation process to evaluate and describe the architecture. The following aspects of the information transmission process must be taken into consideration:

- **Performance**: Indicates how much data can be transmitted reliably per unit of time and which configuration is used.
- **Reliability**: Describes how reliable data can be transmitted without losses, and which methods are used.
- **Resiliency**: Explains how flexible errors in the connection topology are handled and which methods are used. This also includes failover protocols (for example, for clusters).
- **Security**: Indicates how securely data is transmitted, without unauthorized system components or external components having access to the information, and which methods are used.

Transport protocols

The following table gives an overview of the most important transport protocols which are used as building blocks in the communication layer.

Protocol	Description
TCP	The **Transmission Control Protocol** is the most widely used transport protocol. It also forms the basis for other protocols. TCP establishes a failsafe, direct, connection-based communication channel over IP between two endpoints, which are known as **sockets**.
UDP	The **User Datagram Protocol** is a connectionless, non-reliable communication channel between endpoints. In contrast to TCP, the receiver does not notice when data packets go missing. The transmission speed is higher than that of TCP.
FTP	The **File Transfer Protocol** is used to transmit character-based or binary files over TCP/IP.
HTTP	The **Hypertext Transfer Protocol** is a stateless, point-to-point protocol. In addition to being used to call web pages, it also forms the basis for a number of protocols for addressing web services.
IIOP	The **Internet Inter-ORB protocol** is defined in the CORBA standard and is used by distributed **Object Request Brokers** (ORBs) to communicate with one another across the network. This involves methods being called by remote components or objects. IIOP is a specialized version of the abstract **GIOP (General Inter-ORB Protocol)** based on TCP/IP. ORBs from different manufacturers can communicate with one another using IIOP. IIOP is also an alternative communication protocol for RMI.
RMI	The Java **Remote Method Invocation** describes **RPCs (Remote Procedure Calls)** for Java applications, which are the method calls made by an object running in one **JVM (Java Virtual Machine)** to an object running in another. This JVM may also be on a different physical machine. RMI is also the communication protocol for remote calls to Java objects. As an alternative, IIOP can be used, in which case the complete protocol is referred to as RMI over IIOP.
ODBC	**Open Database Connectivity** is a standardized API used as a database interface for applications. Product-specific ODBC drivers are required.
JDBC	**Java Database Connectivity** is a Java EE API specification which gives Java applications standardized access to databases. A JDBC-ODBC bridge allows ODBC databases to be addressed via JDBC. Product-specific JDBC drivers are used to access databases.
JMS	**Java Message Service** is a Java EE API specification for exchanging messages between Java applications. Point-to-point communication is defined on the basis of queues, while publish/subscribe communication is based on topics.

Protocol	Description
SQL*NET/ Net8	This is Oracle client/server middleware, which establishes connections between the client and the database, or between two databases. It is based on **TNS (Transparent Network Substrate).** This is Oracle's network architecture, which provides a standardized API, giving applications transparent access to the lower-level network protocols.
SOAP	**SOAP** is a protocol specification for exchanging structured information in the implementation of Web Services in computer networks. The transport formats are based on XML, and HTTP is generally used as the transport protocol. SOAP forms the foundation layer of a web services protocol stack.
XML-RPC	In historical terms, the **XML Remote Procedure Call** is the predecessor of SOAP. The protocol defines simple XML data containers for transporting information from service providers to service consumers. It is used for synchronous calls from remote service interfaces. It is generally based on HTTP, but JMS and XMPP (Jabber-RPC) can also be used.
MSMQ	**Microsoft Message Queuing** is a queue-based message protocol from Microsoft.
SMTP	The **Simple Mail Transmission Protocol** is used to exchange e-mails.
IMAP	The **Internet Message Access Protocol** is used to download e-mails from a mail server. The mails remain physically on the server.
POP3	The **Post Office Protocol 3** is used to physically download e-mails from a mail server.
XMPP	The **Extensible Messaging and Presence Protocol** allows for real-time communication through XML protocols (referred to as instant messaging). XMPP forms the basis for the widely used Jabber protocol for instant messaging.
NFS	The **Network File System** protocol, originally developed by SUN Microsystems, gives access to files over a network. The files are not transferred in the same way as with FTP, but instead they remain a shared resource on the server. NFS is based on TCP/IP.
SMB	The **Service Message Block** is the Microsoft Windows equivalent of NFS, which comes originally from the Unix world.
iSCSI	The **Internet Small Computer System Interface (iSCSI)** protocol enables clients (referred to here as initiators) to send SCSI commands (known as CDBs) to an SCSI storage device on a remote computer. This is a distributed **SAN (Storage Area Network)** protocol, which creates virtual disk space. iSCSI can be used over longer distances on an existing network infrastructure. In contrast, fiber channel protocols require special cabling.

Protocol	Description
DCOM	The **Distributed Component Object Model** is an object-oriented RPC system, based on the DCEstandard. It was defined by Microsoft to allow COM technology to communicate over a network. Although DCOM was developed by, and is largely used, by Microsoft (for example, ActiveX), there are a range of adapters which make it possible to communicate through DCOM without using DCOM directly.
ADO.NET	**ADO.NET** is part of the Microsoft .NET platform. It consists of a collection of classes which allow access to relational databases. ADO.NET is the successor to **ActiveX Data Objects (ADO)**.

Transport formats

The following table gives an overview of the most important transport formats, which are used as building blocks in the communication layer:

Format	Description
ebXML	ebXML stands for **Electronic Business using XML**. It is not an individual standard, but a family of different standards from UN/CEFACT and OASIS. The ebXML standards include the ebXML Technical Architecture Specification, an XML Business Process Specification Schema, a Registry Services Specification with Registry Information Model (ebRIM), and a Message Service Specification (Patil, Newcomer 2003).
EdiFact	**United Nations Electronic Data Interchange for Administration, Commerce and Transport (EDI, UN/Edifact)** is a global standard which allows the traceable processing of business transactions among companies, or between companies and public authorities using the standardized electronic exchange of data (Grangard et al. 2001).
SWIFT	The **Society for Worldwide Interbank Financial Telecommunications** is a society which supplies telecommunications services between banks all over the world. The term *SWIFT* is also used to refer to the network that the society provides. SWIFT is used to exchange messages between banks (CSSWIFT 2005).
HL7	**Health Level 7** is an international standard for exchanging data between applications and systems in the healthcare sector. It (HL7V3 1998) describes communication at an application level on the basis of level 7 of the ISO/OSI reference model for communication (ISO7498-1).
BAPI	**Business Application Programming Interface** is a standardized programming interface for SAP Business Objects. BAPIs enable external programs to access SAP R/3 data and business processes (Moser 2003).

Format	Description
IDoc	**Intermediate Document** is a SAP format for exchanging data from a business transaction. Different IDoc types are available to support different message types. For example, the IDoc format ORDERS01 can be used for orders and order confirmations (Krawczyk 2006).
AdsML	**Accelerating Advertising Processes in the Digital Age** is a collection of e-commerce standards that support the exchange of business messages using XML in the advertising industry (Brunner 2007).
RosettaNet	Within the RosettaNet organization, user groups and members agree on and standardize open, cross-industry communication and workflow processes for the electronic exchange of business documents between the users' IT systems. This enables suppliers and customers to exchange data with as few media and data conversion problems as possible (B2B). The focus is primarily on logistics and production, but the exchange of product and material data and service processes are also included (Damodaran 2004).

Integration domain level: Collection/distribution layer

The **collection/distribution layer** is part of the **integration domain level** and is responsible for collecting and distributing information. It is completely separate from the main part of the integration domain (mediation). The building blocks in this layer connect the mediation layer above with the communication layer below. The layer is responsible for encapsulating external protocols and their technical details from the integration application, and transforming external formats into familiar internal formats.

Responsibility

The responsibility of the collection/distribution layer is to collect and distribute information.

Concepts and methods

The basic requirements for the implementation of the collection/distribution layer are listed in the following table, along with where in the book to find more information:

Requirement	Section in Chapter 1
Middleware	*Middleware*

The base technologies needed for the implementation of the collection/distribution layer are listed in the following table:

Base technology	Section in Chapter 2
Java Connector Architecture (JCA) as an example of an adapter framework	*Java Connector Architecture (JCA)*
Service Data Objects (SDO) as an example of a Disconnected Data Architecture	*Service Data Objects (SDO)*

Building blocks

The following table gives an overview of the building blocks used in the collection/distribution layer:

Building block	Description
Adapter (or Connector)	Adapters are components, which connect application-specific APIs with the access protocols (or access APIs) of the transport layer components in order to enable them to communicate with the source and target systems. Adapters decouple the applications from the APIs specific to the transport layer, and are usually separated from the application. One example of an adapter is the **Java Connector Architecture (JCA)** (see *Chapter 2*).
Mapper	Mappers encapsulate the logic used to align the formats in the communication infrastructure and the formats in the domain objects. Domain objects and components belonging to the communication infrastructure are decoupled from the mapper, and are unaware of its existence. **Dozer** is a JavaBean to JavaBean mapper that recursively copies data from one bean to another. Typically, these JavaBeans will be of different complex types. **Dozer** supports: • Simple property mapping • Complex types and graphs, bi-directional mapping • Implicit-explicit mapping • Recursive mapping

Building block	Description
Data mapper (or mapper)	The data mapper is a layer of mappers, which transfers data between objects and databases, without making the object and the database dependent on one another, or indeed on the mapper.
	The data mapper is a layer of software that separates the in-memory objects from the database. Its responsibility is to transfer data between the objects and the database, and also to isolate them from each other. With the data mapper, the objects do not even need to know that there is a database present. They do not need SQL interface code or any knowledge of the database schema.
DAO	A **Data Access Object** (**DAO**) is a design pattern that encapsulates the access to different types of data sources (for example, databases, filesystems, and so on) in such a way that the data source that is being addressed can be replaced without changing the calling code. This allows the program logic to be separated from the technical details of the data storage, and makes it more flexible. A **DAO** can also be used as a pattern for designing programming interfaces (APIs).
	When it is implemented, a **DAO** can make use of a data mapper.

Integration domain level: Mediation layer

The **mediation layer** is part of the **integration domain level** and is responsible for forwarding information. It includes the most important functionality of the integration domain. Its main task is to ensure the reliable forwarding of information to business components in the process layer, or directly to building blocks in the collection/distribution layer. In more complex scenarios, the information forwarding process can be enhanced by information transformation and filtering, and so on.

Responsibility

The responsibility of the mediation layer is to forward information.

Chapter 3

Concepts and methods

The basic requirements for the implementation of the mediation layer are listed in the following table, along with where in the book to find more information.

Requirement	Section of Chapter 1
Messaging, publish/subscribe, message brokers, and messaging infrastructure	*Messaging*
	Publish/subscribe
	Message broker
	Messaging infrastructure
ESB	*Enterprise Service Bus (ESB)*
Point-to-point, hub-and-spoke, pipeline, and Service-Oriented Architectures	*Integration architecture variants*
Federation, population, and synchronization	*Data integration*
Direct connections, broker, and router	*EAI/EII*

The base technologies needed for the implementation of the mediation layer are listed in the following table:

Base technology	Section of Chapter 2
OSGi	*OSGi*
Java Business Integration (JBI) as a sample ESB implementation	*Java Business Integration (JBI)*
Service Component Architecture (SCA) as a sample component framework	*Service Component Architecture (SCA)*

Building blocks

The following building blocks are used in the mediation layer:

Canonical data model

One problem that occurs in many integration scenarios, is the need to map external data formats from several different source systems onto the internal data formats of many different target applications. In the case of a point-to-point approach, each combination would have to be mapped individually.

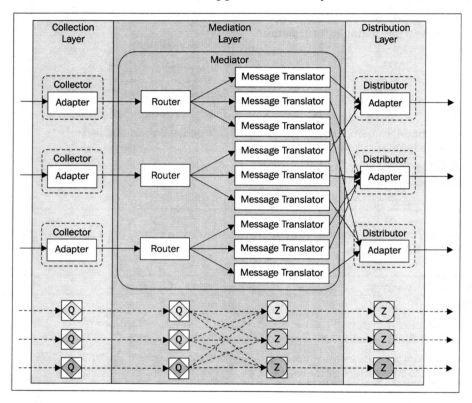

The problem can be resolved by introducing a general format, which is used in the integration solution and in all new target applications. Only one mapping to this internal format needs to be maintained for the existing applications. This keeps maintenance and development costs to a minimum. Internal formats of this kind are referred to as **canonical formats**. In the context of ESB, the term **normalized message format** is also used.

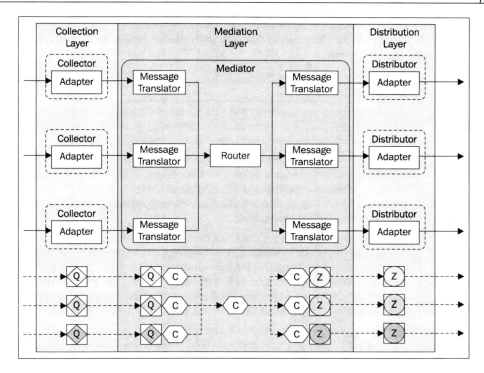

Canonical data models are independent of any specific application. Each application is decoupled from other formats and only needs to be able to generate and read the canonical format. Application-specific components that implement the message translator pattern are used for this purpose.

A canonical data model reduces the number of message translators needed, as only one is required for each application.

One single canonical data model does not always have to cover the whole enterprise. It's definitely valid, and often even better, to start small and to only concentrate on a subset of the data within an enterprise, often on so-called **domain levels**. The result of this is to have different and independent canonical data models, each with a domain specific scope. Such a canonical data model can be seen as a domain-specific view on the enterprise-wide data model.

In an environment where multiple ESBs are used on different levels (using the federated ESB pattern), it's also possible to have different canonical models on each level, that is a **federated canonical data model** message endpoint.

This group of patterns connects applications to messaging systems. The building blocks are listed in the following table, though only those patterns that are frequently used in practice are described:

Building Block	Description
Message endpoint	An application is connected to a message channel through a message endpoint. This is a client of the messaging system and the application can send and receive messages via this message endpoint.
Polling consumer	A polling consumer sends a call to the messaging system only when the application wants to receive a message. This is also referred to as a **synchronous receiver**, as the receiver is blocked until the message is received. The receiver polls for a message, processes it, and then polls for the next message.
Event-driven consumer	An event-driven consumer is a component that is called by the messaging system when a new message arrives on the consumer channel. Using a callback method in the application API, the event-driven consumer forwards the message to the application. This is also referred to as an **asynchronous receiver**, as the receiver does not have a running thread until the callback thread delivers a message.
Competing consumers	Competing consumers are a group of several potential receivers on a single point-to-point channel. The consumers compete with one another, but only one can process each specific message. This makes it possible to process several messages in parallel.
Message dispatcher	A message dispatcher reads a message from an individual channel and sends it to the correct receiver, where it is processed. The message dispatcher can decide which receiver is appropriate for each message.
Selective consumer	Selective consumers filter the messages arriving in the channel and receive only those messages which fulfill the selection criteria.

Message construction

This group of patterns is responsible for sending messages using channels, the details of which are listed in the table below. Note that only those patterns which are frequently used in practice are described.

Building Block	Description
Request/reply	Request/reply ensures that an application which sends a message to the messaging system can receive a reply from the receiver. A message request/reply pair is used for this purpose, with each message having its own channel.
Building Block	Description

Return address	In a request/reply scenario, the request message contains the return address, which specifies where the reply message should be sent.
Correlation identifier	Each reply message can contain a correlation identifier (a unique ID), which specifies the request message that the reply refers to.

Messaging channel

This group of patterns relates to different types of channels, and the methods used to connect them to an application. The building blocks are listed in the following table. Only those patterns which are frequently used in practice are described.

Building Block	Description
Point-to-point channel	The use of a point-to-point channel allows the message system to ensure that a message can only be processed by one single receiver.
Publish/subscribe channel	A publish/subscribe channel makes it possible for a message to have several potential receivers. The messaging system ensures that every receiver receives the message once.
Invalid message channel	If a receiver recognizes that a message is incorrect (for example, in its format) or seems to not make sense, it can place the message in an invalid message channel, which is a special channel for messages that the receiver cannot process.
Dead letter channel	If the messaging system recognizes that it is not possible to deliver a message, it can move the message to a dead letter channel. This channel is also referred to as a dead letter queue or dead message queue.
Channel adapter	The channel adapter acts as a client of the messaging system and calls the application via a specific API. This allows every application to be connected to a messaging system and to interact with other applications, providing that a suitable channel adapter is available.

Message routing

This group of patterns enables the sender and the receiver of a message to be more effectively decoupled. The building blocks are listed in the following table. Only those patterns which are frequently used in practice are described.

Building Block	Description
Pipes and filters	Pipes-and-filters is a style of architecture which allows larger processing tasks to be broken down into a sequence of smaller, independent steps (filters) connected through channels (pipes).
Content-based router	A content-based router sends a message to the correct receiver on the basis of its content. The routing process can be based on a range of different criteria, such as the existence of fields or field contents.
Message filter	The message filter is a special type of router. On the basis of a selection of criteria, it removes unwanted messages from a channel. If a message meets the filter criteria, it is forwarded. Otherwise, it is discarded.
Dynamic router	The dynamic router is an additional control channel, which receivers can use to register and identify the messages that they are interested in. The dynamic router stores the receivers' preferences in a rules database.
Recipient list	Each receiver has its own channel. On the basis of the incoming message, the recipient list identifies the list of receiver endpoints and sends the message to all the receivers on the list.
Splitter	A splitter breaks a composite message down into several individual messages, which are subsequently processed independently. The splitter publishes each message individually.
Aggregator	The aggregator is a special message filter. It receives a message stream, identifies the messages which need correlating, correlates them into a single message, and publishes this message on the output channel.
Resequencer	The resequencer can receive a message stream with messages in the wrong order. It has an internal buffer for storing messages that arrive in the wrong order until the correct order is restored.

Message transformation

This group of patterns ensures that applications can interact with one another using the messaging system, despite the fact that they describe data in different ways and use different formats. The building blocks are listed in the following table. Only those patterns which are frequently used in practice are described.

Building Block	Description
Message translator	The message translator is a special message filter that can convert data from one format to another. It is primarily used to ensure that domain objects and the canonical data model have the same format. A translator is a special type of filter.
Content enricher	A content enricher is a special kind of transformer, which can add missing information to a message from an external data source.
Claim check	The claim check stores the message data in persistent storage and only sends a reference to the subsequent components. These components can use the reference to access the stored information. This reduces the volume of data in the messages sent across the system.

Application level: Process layer

The **process layer** is part of the **application level** and is responsible for orchestrating component and service calls. It manages the building blocks in the mediation layer (if they cannot act autonomously). This supports and simplifies the implementation of complex integration processes.

Responsibility

The responsibility of the process layer is to manage and control the building blocks in the mediation layer.

Concepts and methods

The basic requirements for the implementation of the process layer are listed in the following table, along with where in the book to find more information:

Requirement	Section of Chapter 1
SOA	*Service-oriented integration*
Event-driven architecture	*Event-driven architecture*
Complex event processing	*Complex event processing*
	XTP and CEP

Integration Architecture Blueprint

The base technologies needed for the implementation of the process layer are listed in the following table.

Base technology	Section of Chapter 2
Service Component Architecture (SCA)	*Service Component Architecture (SCA)*
Process modeling	*Process modeling*

Building blocks

The following building blocks are used in the process layer:

Job scheduler

Job schedulers manage, automate, monitor, and plan dependencies between programs. Jobs and programs are started and made dependent on one another across different computers under the control of the scheduler, which allows complex dependencies to be created.

The basic features of a job scheduler are as follows:

- An interface for defining jobs, workflows, and dependencies between jobs
- Automatically starting jobs
- An interface for monitoring and troubleshooting jobs
- Priorities and/or queues to control the execution order of unrelated jobs

Most operating systems provide basic job-scheduling capabilities, such as **cron**, which runs on Unix. Job schedulers also form part of database, ERP, and business process management systems. However, these often do not meet the complex requirements of enterprise job scheduling. In this case, it is worth installing specific job scheduler software, such as **Cronacle**, **IBM Tivioli Workload Scheduler**, **Open Source Job Scheduler**, or **Quartz**.

Portal

In the IT world, the term **portal** is used to describe a central point of access which makes customized, internal and external information and services available. The focus is on the provision of cross-application services (in other words, integration) and not on the technical (for example, web-based) implementation.

Workflow

A workflow, which is an executable process, is by far the most important building block in the process layer. Workflow building blocks form the basis for implementing the technical processes that control an integration solution. They can be implemented, for example, in **Business Process Execution Language** (**BPEL**) using a BPEL engine. All the workflow building blocks can be created using BPEL.

The following table gives an overview of the building blocks used to produce workflows:

Building block	Description
Basic control patterns	
Sequence	Executes one or more activities in sequence.
Parallel split	Executes two or more activities in sequence or in parallel.
Synchronization	Synchronizes two or more activities running in sequence or in parallel. Waits to continue until all the previous activities have been completed. Also known as barrier synchronization.
Exclusive choice	One of several execution paths is selected, on the basis of information which must be available at the time when the exclusive choice activity is executed.
Simple merge	Waits to complete one of several activities before continuing with processing. The assumption is that only one of these activities is executed. This is generally because these activities are on different paths, based on an exclusive choice or deferred choice.
Advanced branching and synchronization patterns	
Multiple choice	Selects several execution paths from a number of alternatives.
Synchronizing merge	Brings together several execution paths and synchronizes them, if several paths were in use. Performs the same role as the simple merge, if only one execution path was in use.
Multiple merge	A point in a workflow process where two or more paths are merged without being synchronized. If more than one path was activated, then after the merge, one activity is started for each incoming path.
Discriminator	A point in the workflow process that waits for one of the incoming paths to be completed before activating the next activity. From that moment on, the discriminator waits for all the remaining paths to be completed, but ignores the results. After all the incoming paths have been activated, the pattern is reset and can be reactivated. (This is important, because it could not otherwise be used in a loop.)

Advanced branching and synchronization patterns	
N-out-of-M join	Similar to the discriminator pattern, but this pattern makes it possible to wait for more than one preceding activity (**N**) which is to be completed, and then to continue with the next activity. The subsequent activity is only activated when the N paths have been completed.
Structural patterns	
Arbitrary cycles	A point in the workflow where one or more activities are executed several times.
Implicit termination	Terminates a process instance when there is no more to be done.
Multiple instances (MI) patterns	
Multiple instances without synchronization	Several instances of an activity are created for one process instance and each is executed in a separate thread. No synchronization takes place.
Multiple instances with a priori known design time knowledge	Several instances of an activity are created for one process instance. The number of instances of a given activity is known at design time.
Multiple instances with a priori known runtime time knowledge	Several instances of an activity are created for one process instance, but the number of instances is not known until runtime. At a specific point during runtime, the number can be determined (as in a FOR loop, but with parallel processing).
Multiple instances without a priori runtime knowledge	Several instances of an activity are created for one process instance, but the number of instances is not known at design time. Even at runtime it is not clear how many instances will finally be needed until the activities are established. The difference between this and the previous pattern is that after the parallel instances have been completed, or when instances are still being executed, additional, new instances of an activity can be created at any time.
State-based patterns	
Deferred choice	Executes one of several alternative paths. The alternative to be executed is not selected on the basis of the data available at the time of the deferred choice, but is determined by an event (for example, when an end user chooses a task from a work-list).
Interleaved parallel routing	Executes a number of activities in random order, possibly depending on the availability of resources. The order is not known until runtime and none of the activities are executed at the same time (in other words, in parallel).
Milestone	An activity is only executed when the process has a specific status, in other words, a specific milestone has been reached. Otherwise, the activity is not activated.

Cancellation patterns	
Cancel activity	Stops an active activity that is being executed.
Cancel case	Stops an entire active process.

Event processing pattern

The most commonly used CEP technology patterns are described here to provide support for the implementation of integration solutions based on an event-driven architecture (Coral8 2007).

- **Filtering**: A simple pattern for filtering events out of one or more event streams. A filter expression is applied to the incoming events and if the condition is `true`, the event is published in the output stream.

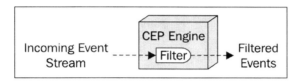

- **In-memory caching**: This pattern keeps events in memory, for example for a time-based window covering the last 10 minutes. This forms the basis for many other CEP design patterns.

    The cache typically stores two kinds of data:
    - Recent events from one or more input streams
    - Data from one or more database tables

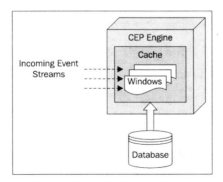

- **Aggregation over windows**: Computes statistics over different types of sliding windows (for example, a time-based window covering the last 10 minutes or an event-based window with the last 10 events).

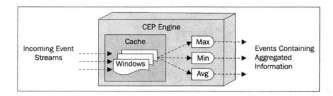

- **Database lookups**: Accessing databases to compare historical information or references with incoming events.

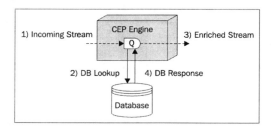

- **Database writes**: Sending raw or derived events to a database.

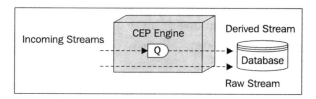

- **Correlation (joins)**: Joining multiple event streams.

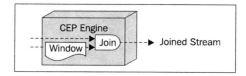

- **Event pattern matching**: Complex time-based patterns of events across multiple streams.

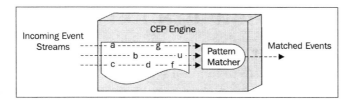

- **State machines**: Modeling complex behavior and processes through state machines.

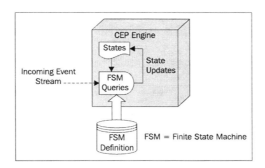

- **Hierarchical events**: Processing, analyzing and composing hierarchical events.

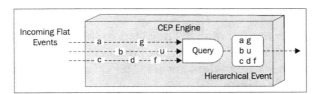

- **Dynamic queries**: Submitting parameterized queries, requests and subscriptions dynamically.

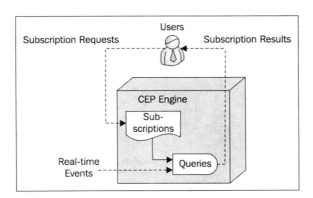

Integration Architecture Blueprint

Notation and visualization

Notation and visualization describes a notation, which makes it easy to visualize example scenarios in the blueprint. This section forms the foundation for the next chapter of this book, which uses individual scenarios to show how the fundamental patterns from *Chapter 1* can be implemented with the integration blueprint.

Representing the scenarios and the notation used

Dynamic aspects are represented in scenarios, as shown in the following example:

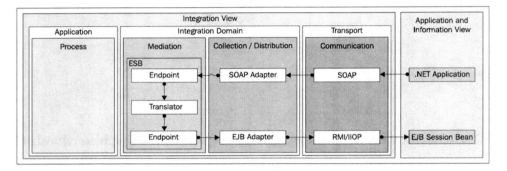

Scenarios are read from top to bottom. They start in the top-right corner with an information source system. The target system of the integration process, or of an individual step, is in the bottom-right corner. The valid notation elements are shown in the following diagram:

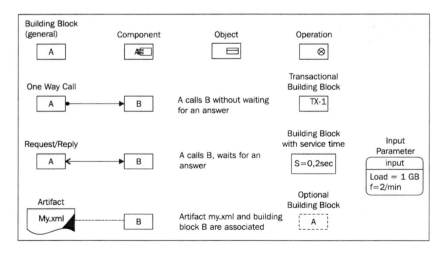

In the image above, a .NET application sends a web service call through SOAP using one-way call semantics, which means that it does not expect a reply. The query passes through an SOAP adapter and causes an ESB service to start, which receives the query as a message. The message is transformed in a translator building block and an EJB (Enterprise JavaBean) adapter is used to connect to an EJB session bean, which is also called using a one-way call. In other words, this integration solution makes it possible to use an EJB session bean from a .NET application through a simple, standards-compliant web service request.

In this example, the optional process layer is not used, as no additional management activities are needed. The management role is performed by the source .NET application.

Visualizing different levels of granularity

In the diagrams, the general building block is used most frequently. However, it may be advisable to choose building blocks with different levels of granularity for visualization purposes. The blueprint provides components (coarse granular notation elements), objects (medium granularity), and operations (fine granular elements). One example of their use can be seen in the following image:

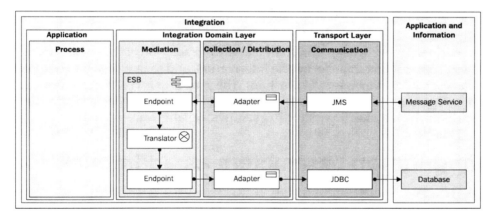

It is clear that an adapter is an object. In an actual implementation, this could be a Java or a .NET object, for example. The ESB building block is shown as a component that contains other building blocks, and among these is the translator building block that is designated as an operation. In an implementation, this can take the form of one or multiple methods of a class or a module (for example, Oracle PL/SQL package).

Representing transaction boundaries

Representing transaction boundaries is important for the purposes of planning and describing the required system behavior. Each building block is given the label **TX-n**, where TX stands for **transaction** and n is a unique identifier which specifies that the building block belongs to the transaction with this ID. This enables even nested transactions to be represented. The following diagram shows a sample scenario with such a transaction:

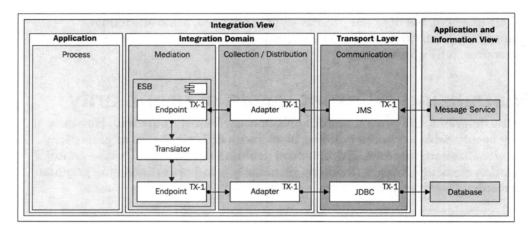

This scenario shows an integration solution which reads from a JMS queue via an adapter in a transaction, transforms the information, and then writes the data via JDBC to a database table (in the same transaction). The source only considers a message to have been processed if it was successfully written to the database table (using an XA transaction), which makes it possible to guarantee reliable transmission.

Configuration parameters as additional artifacts

The scenario in the preceding diagram is dependent on some corresponding configuration parameters (for example, for EJB components among others). This information can also be expressed using additional artifacts, as shown in the following diagram:

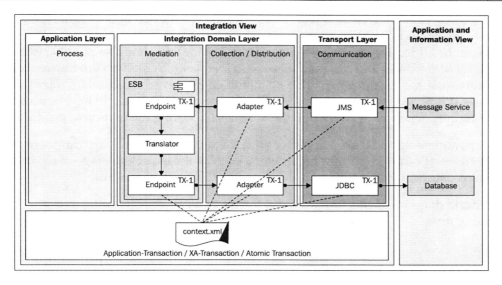

Extension for capacity planning

When integrating larger volumes of data (for example in ETL scenarios), it is advisable to identify possible bottlenecks at an early stage of the process of capacity planning and SLA definition. Quantitative scenarios can be helpful in this respect, as shown in the following diagram:

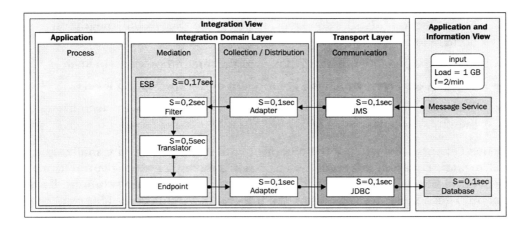

The building blocks are labeled with service times. The service time indicates how quickly information must pass through the building block, and the individual service times can be added together to give the overall service time. It is also possible to make estimates of the times and compare them with load tests. In modern environments, the individual service times can often be identified relatively accurately. Quantitative analysis at unit test level can also be used to determine the service times. The accuracy of the figures depends, of course, on the facilities for testing the platform/product.

Input parameters can be used together with the service times to carry out theoretical calculations of other important parameters, such as the expected usage of a particular resource. The example is based on a data load of 2 x 1 GB per minute.

A scenario diagram of this kind can also form a base for documenting and planning tests.

Summary

You have now finished the most important chapter of this book. At this point in time, you should know what the Trivadis Integration Architecture Blueprint is, how it is structured into different layers, and why it has been defined this way. You should now be familiar with:

- The information flow and the mutual dependencies between the components of the blueprint
- The communication layer, which is part of the integration domain level
- The collection/distribution layer, which forms part of the integration domain level
- The mediation layer, which belongs to the integration domain level
- The process layer, which is a component of the application level
- The notation and visualization, which can be used to easily visualize integration scenarios

In the next chapter, we will use the blueprint with its notation and visualization to visualize some common integration scenarios in a mostly product-neutral form. We will cover traditional, as well as modern, SOA-driven integration solutions. By then you should get a better feeling of how the Integration Architecture Blueprint can be used in practice.

Implementation scenarios

Having understood the business patterns described in *Chapter 1, Basic Principles*, and the structure of the blueprint covered in *Chapter 3, Integration Architecture Blueprint*, this chapter will use individual scenarios to illustrate how the business pattern can be implemented using the Integration Architecture Blueprint.

The scenarios have been deliberately designed to be independent of specific vendor products, and are based solely on the building blocks that form part of the different layers of the blueprint.

The symbols used have the same semantic meaning as described in *Chapter 3*.

This chapter will:

- Explain service-oriented integration scenarios
- Use scenarios to show how data integration business patterns can be implemented
- Present a description of scenarios for implementing the business patterns for EAI/EII integration
- Look in detail at the implementation of event processing business patterns
- Describe a scenario for implementing business patterns for grid computing and **Extreme Transaction Processing (XTP)**
- Explain how an SAP ERP system can be combined with the integration blueprint
- Explain how an existing integration solution can be modernized using SOA, and describe a scenario that has already been implemented in practice
- Combine the integration blueprint with the other Trivadis Architecture Blueprints

EAI/EII scenarios

These scenarios show how the EAI/EII integration business patterns described in *Chapter 1* can be implemented. These business patterns are as follows:

- **Direct connection**: Represents the simplest type of interaction between two applications and is based on a 1:1 topology, in other words, an individual point-to-point connection.
- **Broker**: Is based on the direct connection pattern and extends it to a 1: N topology. It allows an individual query from a source application to be routed to several target applications.
- **Router**: A variant of the broker pattern with several potential target applications, where the message is routed to only one target application.

Implementing the direct connection business pattern

An SOA-based implementation of the direct connection business pattern makes use of an ESB component in the mediation layer, as shown in the following diagram:

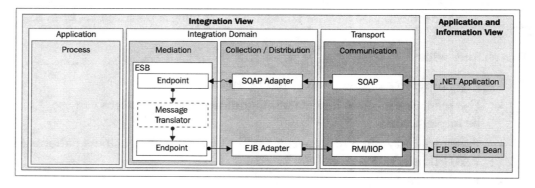

Trigger:

    An application sends a request using a web service.

Primary flow:

1. An endpoint on the ESB receives the request through SOAP from the calling application and sends it as a message in a channel on the bus.
2. The message uses the second endpoint and the EJB adapter to call an EJB session bean.

Alternative flows:

- The calls can use request/reply instead of one-way semantics and return a result to the calling application.
- A message translator building block can be used to transform the message (data mapping).

Variant with synchronous call over asynchronous protocol

A variant of the previous scenario is that of bridging from a synchronous to an asynchronous request and response exchange pattern. This can be helpful if the target system is only accessible through some **message-oriented middleware (MOM)**, that is, a message queue. Asynchronous request-response messaging can be achieved using separate queues: one for the request messages and one for the response messages. Asynchronous request-response messaging is often the best approach for interacting with some mainframe systems, such as IBM zSeries systems through MQSeries. (IBM's message-oriented middleware offering, now also known as Websphere MQ.)

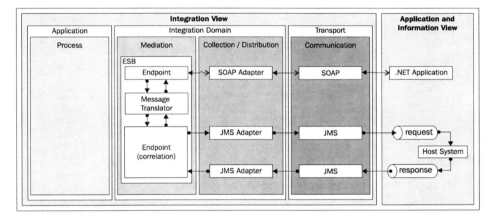

Trigger:

An application sends a request using a web service.

Primary flow:

1. An endpoint on the ESB receives the request through SOAP from the calling application.
2. The message is translated into the format of the target system.

3. The message is placed into the request queue through a JMS adapter, adding some additional information used for correlation.
4. The host system consumes the request message from the queue, processes the request, and sends the response information by placing the message into the response queue, together with the correlation information.
5. The ESB endpoint consumes the response message and uses the correlation information to correlate the response with the corresponding request.
6. The response is translated into the source format and returned as an SOAP response message to the requester.

Implementing the broker business pattern

An SOA-based implementation of the broker business pattern also makes use of an ESB in the mediation layer. This provides support for a **publish/subscribe** pattern, or a **message dispatcher** pattern. The scenario is shown in the following diagram:

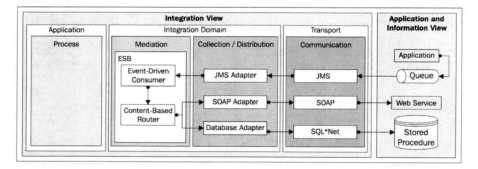

Trigger:

   An application places a message in the queue.

Primary flow:

1. An event-driven consumer building block on the ESB uses the JMS adapter to extract the message from the queue and sends it in a channel on the bus.
2. The message is forwarded by a content-based router building block to the interested systems (there may be more than one). The router bases its activities on the content of the message, in other words, the information in the message header or body.
3. The first system offers a web service interface and can therefore be connected directly through an SOAP adapter.

4. The second system is connected to the database by means of a stored procedure, which is supported by the corresponding database adapter.

Alternative flows:

- The message router can be based on the canonical data model, which means that a message translator building block is incorporated upstream and downstream of the message router building block. First of all, the message is converted into canonical format, then the routing logic is applied to the canonical format, and the message is transformed into the format of the target system before it is forwarded.
- If the routing rules are complex, they can be externalized into an external rule engine.
- The content-based router can be replaced by a dynamic router, which results in a dynamic subscribe mechanism that allows the potential target systems to subscribe dynamically.
- BPEL can be used for the mediation instead of the ESB.

Implementing the router business pattern

An SOA-based implementation of the router business pattern is possible if an ESB is used in the mediation layer. This is shown in the following diagram:

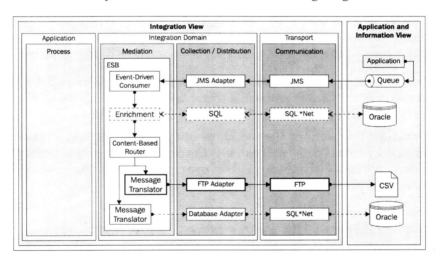

Trigger:

An application places a message in the queue.

Primary flow:

1. An event-driven consumer building block on the ESB removes the message from the queue through the JMS adapter and places it in a channel on the bus.
2. A content-based router identifies, based on the content of the message, one target system, which in this case is either the FTP or Database distributor (for this example, FTP is chosen, which is marked in bold).
3. The message is transformed into the necessary target format by a message translator building block.
4. An FTP adapter writes the message to a file (CSV format) and forwards it to the receiver using the FTP protocol.

Alternative flows:

- The message translator is not needed if the target format is the same as that of the message that triggers the process
- If the routing rules are complex, they can be externalized into an external rule engine
- BPEL can be used for the mediation instead of the ESB

Service-oriented integration scenarios

These scenarios show how the service-oriented integration business patterns described in *Chapter 1* can be implemented. These business patterns are as follows:

- **Process integration**: The process integration pattern extends the 1: N topology of the broker pattern. It simplifies the serial execution of business services, which are provided by the target applications.
- **Workflow integration**: The workflow integration pattern is a variant of the serial process pattern. It extends the capability of simple serial process orchestration to include support for user interaction in the execution of individual process steps.

Implementing the process integration business pattern

In the scenario shown in the following diagram, the process integration business pattern is implemented using BPEL.

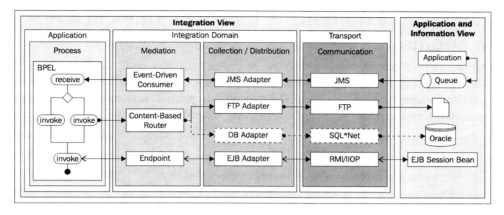

Trigger:

    An application places a message in the queue.

Primary flow:

1. The message is extracted from the queue through JMS and a corresponding JMS adapter.
2. A new instance of the BPEL integration process is started and the message is passed to the instance as input.
3. The integration process orchestrates the integration and calls the systems that are to be integrated in the correct order.
4. A content-based router in the mediation layer is responsible for ensuring that the correct one of the two systems is called. However, from a process perspective, this is only one stage of the integration.
5. In the final step, a "native" integration of an EJB session bean is carried out using an EJB adapter.

Variant with externalized business rules in a rule engine

A variant of the previous scenario has the business rules externalized in a rule engine, in order to simplify the condition logic in the integration process. This corresponds to the external business rules variant of the process integration business pattern, and is shown in the form of a scenario in the following diagram:

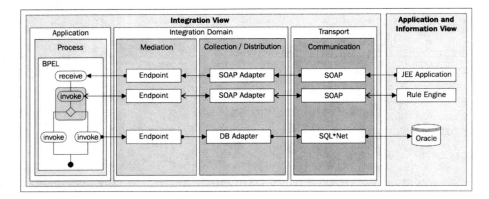

Trigger:

The JEE application sends an SOAP request.

Primary flow:

1. The SOAP request initiates a new instance of the integration process.
2. The integration process is implemented as before, with the exception that in this case, a rule engine is integrated before evaluating the condition. The call to the rule engine from BEPL takes the form of a web service call through SOAP.
3. Other systems can be integrated via a DB adapter as shown here, for example to enable them to write to a table in an Oracle database.

Variant with batch-driven integration process

In this variant, the integration process is initiated by a time-based event. In this case, a job scheduler added before the BPEL process triggers an event at a specified time, which starts the process instance. The process is started by the scheduler via a web service call. The following diagram shows the scenario:

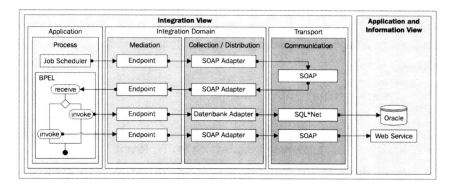

Trigger:

    The job scheduler building block does a web service request at a specified time.

Primary flow:

1. The call from the job scheduler via SOAP initiates a new integration process instance.
2. As in the previous variants, the BPEL process executes the necessary integration steps and, depending on the situation, integrates one system via a database adapter, and the other directly via a web service call.

Implementing the workflow business pattern

In this scenario, additional user interaction is added to the integration process scenario. As a result, the integration process is no longer fully automated. It is interrupted at a specific point by interaction with the end user, for example to obtain confirmation for a certain procedure. This scenario is shown in the following diagram:

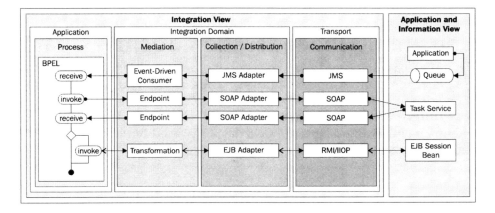

Trigger:

>An application places a message in the queue.

Primary flow:

1. The message is removed from the queue by the JMS adapter and a new instance of the integration process is started.
2. The user interaction takes place through the asynchronous integration of a task service. It creates a new task, which is displayed in the user's task list.
3. As soon as the user has completed the task, the task service returns a callback to the relevant instance of the integration process, and by that, informs the process of the user's decision.
4. The integration process responds to the decision and executes the remaining steps.

Data integration scenarios

These scenarios show how the data integration business patterns described in *Chapter 1* can be implemented. These business patterns are as follows:

- **Federation**: The federation pattern allows access to different data sources, and gives the impression to the requesting application that these are a single logical data source.
- **Population**: The population pattern gathers data from one or more data sources, processes the data in an appropriate way, and applies it to a target database.
- **Synchronization**: The synchronization pattern enables bidirectional update flows of data in multi-copy database environments.

Implementing the federation business pattern

A modern SOA-based approach can be taken in order to implement the federation business pattern. A combination of **splitter** and **aggregator** building blocks from the mediation layer are used to access data from different sources and to bring the data together to form a view. The necessary building blocks are made available by an ESB component. The following diagram shows the SOA-based implementation of the federation business pattern.

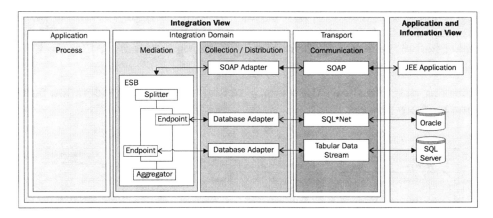

Trigger:

>The application sends a web service request through an SOAP.

Primary flow:

1. The request causes processing to start on the ESB.
2. The ESB splits the request into the number of source systems that are to be used.
3. A request takes place for each source system; in this case, using a database adapter, once for Oracle and once for SQL server.
4. The results of the two requests are combined by the ESB using an aggregator building block to form a single result view, and this result is then returned to the calling application.

Alternative flow:

- The accesses to the source systems can be run in parallel by the ESB in order to keep the overall response time to a minimum (from the perspective of the calling application)

Variant of the federation pattern using mashup technology

Modern mashup techniques from Web 2.0 can be regarded as another way of implementing the federation business pattern.

Mashup refers to the creation of new content by seamlessly (re)combining existing content such as text, data, images, audio, or video, to produce a type of collage. Mashups often make use of application programming interfaces (APIs) made available by other web applications.

The following diagram shows the scenario of implementing the federation pattern using the mashup process:

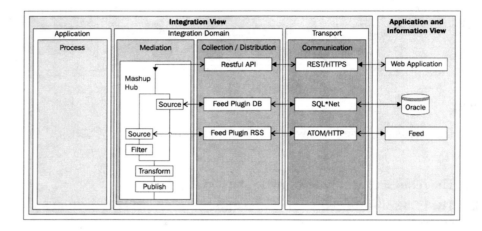

Trigger:

An application sends a request in a **RESTful** style.

Primary flow:

1. The request is received by the mashup server and a processing pipeline is started.
2. The first data source is an Oracle table, which makes information available as a feed through a SQL connection.
3. The second source involves a direct connection to an RSS feed using the **ATOM** protocol, which also returns a feed.
4. The two feeds are combined into one single feed, by using a transform operation (in an aggregator building block).
5. The result is returned to the requesting application using a publish operation.

Implementing the population business pattern

The scenario in the following diagram is the traditional implementation of the population business pattern. This involves using a component that supports ETL functionality and is started at a specific time using a job scheduler building block.

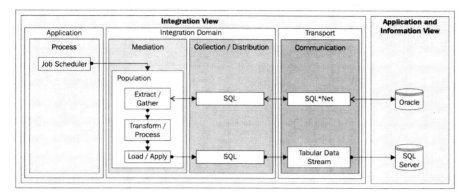

Trigger:

>   The job scheduler building block initiates processing at a given time, determined by the job configuration.

Primary flow:

1. The start event launches the procedure.
2. The extract/gather building block reads the required data from the source, which in this case is an Oracle database.
3. The transform/process building block transforms and processes the data.
4. The load/apply building block writes the data to the target database, which in this case is a SQL Server database.

Variant involving encapsulation of the population pattern as a web service

The population pattern can also be used effectively in a modern SOA-based environment. In this case, the component with the ETL functionality (population) is encapsulated as a web service and incorporated into an SOA. This enables the population pattern to be used by an integration process, as shown in the following diagram:

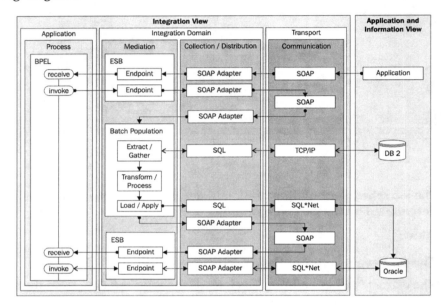

Trigger:

   The application sends a web service request using SOAP.

Primary flow:

1. The SOAP request initiates a new instance of the integration process.
2. To enable the integration process to make use of updated data at a later time, it starts the population procedure via the web service interface, in other words, using an SOAP request, and interrupts/pauses the process.
3. The population procedure (ETL processing) is executed and the data is copied from the DB2 database to the Oracle database using the SQL interfaces.

Chapter 4

4. The integration process is informed that the ETL processing has come to an end by means of an SOAP (callback) request. The process waits for the message with the corresponding receive activity.
5. The process restarts and reads the data from the updated source using a database adapter.

Variant of the population pattern started by a change event from Change Data Capture (CDC)

In the third variant, the population pattern is also used with an SOA-based approach. However, the population procedure is not triggered by a process, but by a change event from the database.

The **Change Data Capture** (**CDC**) method is applied to the source database. CDC has a number of ways of recognizing changes in a source table, for example using database triggers, time stamps or version numbers, or by scanning the database log. Every change identified is published as a CDC event, which a given system can react on. The following image shows the scenario of the event being processed by an ESB, which triggers the population procedure.

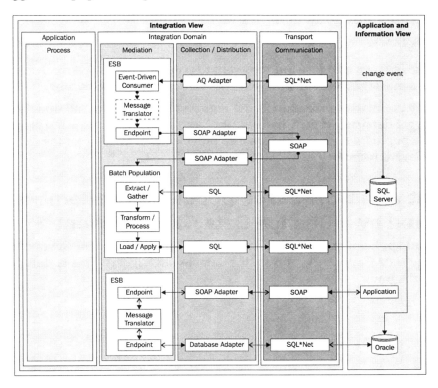

[153]

Implementation scenarios

Trigger:

> A change event from CDC indicates a change in the data (in Oracle database A).

Primary flow:

1. The event is published and forwarded through Oracle Advanced Queuing (AQ), a message infrastructure in the Oracle database.
2. An event-driven consumer in the ESB extracts the message (event) from the database queue using an AQ adapter.
3. If necessary, the ESB transforms the data from a specific format to a canonical format and forwards the event to the required receiver (message dispatcher). In this case, the CDC event causes the population pattern or the ETL processing to start.
4. The population procedure writes the modified data from the source database (Oracle A), to the target database (Oracle B), and transforms the information. As a result, the information is immediately updated in the target database.
5. At any time, the application can access the current data in the target database via a web service query from the ESB mediation layer. The ESB uses a database adapter for the SQL access.

Alternative flows:

- The ESB can also forward the event to potential interested receivers by means of a message router (message dispatcher or publish/subscribe).
- The population procedure is not required to carry out a full update of the target database. If the Change Data Capture event contains the primary key, the population procedure can also only be implemented for the relevant records.

Variant with SOA-based population pattern triggered by a Change Data Capture event

This variant applies a modern SOA-based approach using an ESB component, and the Change Data Capture event from the database as triggers. This is shown in the following diagram:

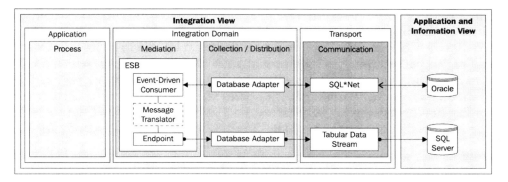

Trigger:

    A record is added or modified in the source Oracle database.

Primary flow:

1. The modification in the database is identified by the database adapter using a specific strategy, such as polling a timestamp column (in principle, a variant of Change Data Capture).
2. An event-driven consumer building block in the ESB reacts to the new or modified record in the source database.
3. The information from the modified record is read and published on the bus as a message in a channel.
4. A message translator building block can be used to convert the message, if required.
5. A database adapter writes the message to the target database (SQL Server).

Implementing the synchronization business pattern

This implementation of the synchronization pattern makes use of the SOA-based implementation of the population pattern. It duplicates this implementation and applies it in both directions. In other words, two parallel, separate message flows are used on the ESB, and both are implemented as a population pattern, as shown in the following diagram.

Implementation scenarios

The important factor in this scenario is to avoid endless loops. This is because the synchronization in one direction represents an update to the target system, which means that the Change Data Capture procedure must be able to process it. One variant of this pattern involves only certain areas of the source data, which do not overlap in the two source databases (for example, at a client level or a regional level) being modified. Another variant labels updates resulting from the synchronization with a flag or a timestamp in every record, so that the Change Data Capture mechanism can distinguish such updates from "normal" application updates.

In addition, this scenario can lead to conflicts if the same record is modified at the same time in both databases. A cleaning process must be put in place when updates to identical records are possible.

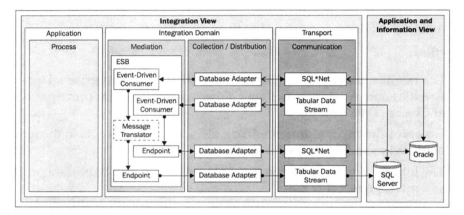

Trigger:

> A record is added or modified in the Oracle or SQL Server database.

Primary flow:

1. One database adapter is used for each database to identify modified or new records by means of a polling procedure. If a change is identified, and if it has been made by a user and not by the synchronization process, then the record is sent as a message in a channel on the bus.
2. The ESB can carry out an optional transformation, and thus writes the record to the target database through a database adapter.

Alternative flow:

- In order to avoid conflicts, the two message flows on the ESB can communicate with one another.

EDA scenario

This scenario shows how the event processing business pattern for event-driven architecture integration described in *Chapter 1* can be implemented.

Implementing the event processing business pattern

As shown in the following diagram, the event processing business pattern can be implemented using a **Complex Event Processing (CEP)** engine, which is controlled by an ESB.

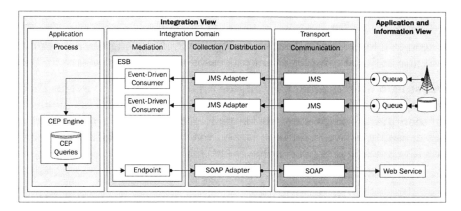

Trigger:

> An event occurs and is placed in a queue by the source system.

Primary flow:

1. An event-driven consumer building block removes the messages or events from the queues using an appropriate JMS adapter, and forwards them to the CEP engine.
2. The CEP engine uses a specific query language to identify the events that are of interest, and enables events to be, for example, filtered, correlated, and aggregated.
3. The CEP engine sends the events that it has identified, in the form of messages, to the ESB endpoint. This ensures that the events are forwarded as messages to a web service through SOAP.
4. The events that are not of interest are discarded.

Implementation scenarios

Alternative flows:

- Events are sent via sources other than queues and are linked to the ESB using the appropriate adapters.
- The events identified as interesting by the CEP engine are sent to a **message router** building block in the mediation layer, which ensures that several potential systems receive the event (in combination with the **broker** business pattern).
- Events that are not of interest are saved in persistent storage.

Variant with two levels of complex event processing

The event processing business pattern can be implemented on more than one level with multiple use of a **CEP engine**, as shown in the following diagram. The **CEP engine** is seen as a logical entity, but in reality, the multiple engines are often the same physical engine with the complex event processor simply being used more than once.

The output stream from the first CEP engine (in other words, the events that are identified) acts as the input stream for the next CEP engine. This makes the process of identifying complex events simpler, as the first CEP query, for example, establishes causality between the events, and the second CEP query aggregates the two events into a new event (a complex event).

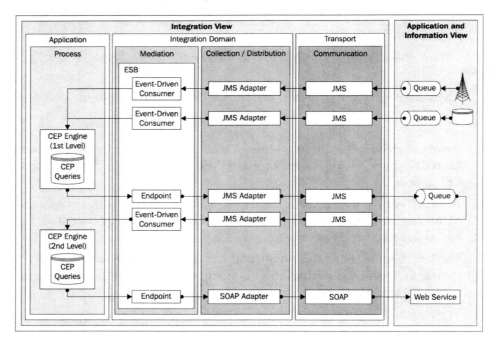

Trigger:

> An event occurs and is placed in a queue by the source system.

Primary flow:

1. An event-driven consumer building block removes the messages or events from the queues using an appropriate JMS adapter and forwards them to the CEP engine.
2. The first CEP engine (first level) defines the events of interest using the query language and places them in another queue.
3. The second CEP engine (second level) uses the second queue as input, and processes the output from the first engine for a second time.
4. The second CEP engine sends the events that it has identified to the ESB endpoint, which ensures that the events are forwarded to a web service through SOAP.
5. The events that are not of interest are discarded.

Alternative flows:

- For reasons of efficiency, an in-memory queue, or a data grid framework (see next section), can be used for the second queue.
- Further levels of CEP engines can be added to identify more complex events, and their causality.
- The CEP engine for each level can take the form of an independent physical engine in order to allow for the processing of a heavy event load.

Grid computing/XTP scenario

This scenario shows how the business pattern for grid computing and **Extreme Transaction Processing (XTP)** technologies described in *Chapter 1* can be implemented.

Implementing the grid computing business pattern

The grid computing business pattern can be implemented using a data grid framework and is shown in the following diagram:

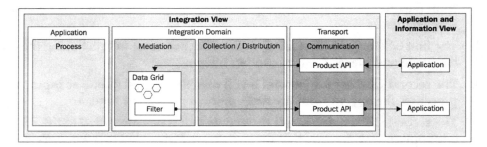

Trigger:

    An application makes a change to an object in the distributed cache.

Primary flow:

1. The data grid ensures that the modified object in the distributed cache is updated.
2. The relevant backup data is updated.
3. Depending on the topology of the cache, the data may be distributed across the entire cluster or only across certain computers.
4. Applications can register their interest on changes to data by applying a suitable filter. In this case, they receive an event whenever the data has been changed.

Variant with ESB wrapping a data grid to cache service results

The grid computing business pattern can be combined with the direct connection pattern and the ESB building block to implement a caching of service results, as shown in the following diagram:

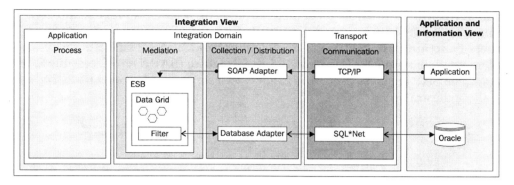

Trigger:

An application sends an SOAP request to the ESB.

Primary flow:

1. The ESB checks if the requested information is already available in the data grid/cache.
2. If the information is available in the cache, then the data is directly returned from the cache.
3. If the information is not in the cache, then the data is read through the database adapter from an Oracle database, placed in the cache, and returned to the requesting application.

Connecting to an SAP system

This scenario shows how SAP can be integrated using the Trivadis Integration Architecture Blueprint. We are making an exception in this case by considering a specific product as a candidate for integration, identifying the corresponding integration platforms, and including them in the scenario. By doing this, we can show how the Integration Architecture Blueprint is used in practice, using some vendor products for the building blocks.

Implementation scenarios

The image below shows how an orchestration using Microsoft BizTalk and SAP can be combined. On the one hand, a simple SAP service is accessed using a **Remote Function Call** (**RFC**), and on the other hand, an SAP business process is implemented using the **SAP Exchange Infrastructure** (**SAP XI**) to access the SAP system. The SAP business process is callable as a service and is used from the BizTalk orchestration.

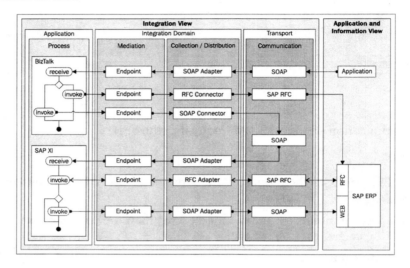

Trigger:

The application sends an SOAP request.

Primary flow:

1. The SOAP request initiates a new instance of a BizTalk process.
2. The process either implements a call directly in SAP in the form of an SAP RFC call, or starts another business process which is made available by SAP XI through an SOAP call.
3. The SAP XI business process is initiated and sends two calls to the SAP system. One takes the form of a SAP RFC call, and the other uses a web service interface made available by SAP.

Modernizing an integration solution

This section uses an example to illustrate how an existing integration solution that has grown over time can be modernized using SOA methods, and the scenarios from the previous sections.

The example is a simplified version of a specific customer project in which an existing solution was modernized with the help of SOA.

The task of the integration solution is to forward orders entered in the central ERP system to the external target applications.

Initial situation

The current solution is primarily based on a file transfer mechanism that sends the new and modified orders at intervals to the relevant applications, in the form of files in two possible formats (XML und CSV). The applications are responsible for processing the files independently.

At a later date, another application (IT App in the following diagram) was added to the system using a queuing mechanism, because this mechanism allowed for the guaranteed exchange of messages with the application by reading new orders, and sending appropriate messages through the queue in the form of a transaction.

The following diagram shows the initial situation before the modernization process took place:

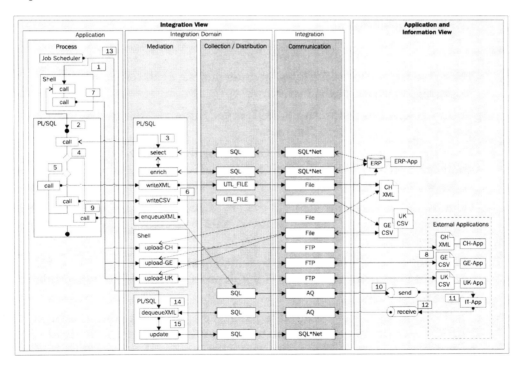

Implementation scenarios

The extraction and file creation logic is written in PL/SQL. A Unix shell script is used to send the files through the **File Transfer Protocol** (**FTP**), as no direct FTP call was possible in PL/SQL. Both a shell script and the PL/SQL logic are responsible for orchestrating the integration process.

Oracle Advanced Queuing (**AQ**) is used as the queuing infrastructure. As PL/SQL supports sending of AQ messages through an API (package), it was possible to implement this special variant of the business case entirely in PL/SQL, without a call to a shell script being needed. In this case, the integration is bi-directional. This means that when the order has been processed by the external system, the application must send a feedback message to the ERP system. A second queue, which is implemented in the integration layer using PL/SQL, is used for this purpose.

Sending new orders

New orders added to the master system (ERP-App) are periodically sent to interested external systems.

Trigger:

> The job scheduler triggers an event every 30 minutes for each external system that has to be integrated.

Flow:

1. The event triggered by the job scheduler starts a shell script, which is responsible for part of the orchestration.
2. The shell script first starts a PL/SQL procedure that creates the files, or writes the information to the queue.
3. The PL/SQL procedure reads all the new orders from the ERP system's database, and enriches them with additional information about the product ordered and the customer.
4. Depending on the external target system, a decision is made as to whether the information about the new order should be sent in the form of files, or messages in queues.
5. The target system can determine in which format (XML or CSV) the file should be supplied. A different PL/SQL procedure is called depending on the desired format.
6. The PL/SQL procedure writes the file in the appropriate format using a PL/SQL tool (in other words, the built-in package UTL_FILE) to the database server. The database server is used only for interim storage of the files, as these are uploaded to the target systems in the next step.

7. The main shell script starts the process of uploading the files to the external system, and another shell script completes the task.
8. The files are made available on the external system and are processed in different ways depending on the application in question.
9. A PL/SQL procedure is called to send the order information through the queue. The procedure is responsible for formatting and sending the message.
10. The document is now in the output queue (*send*) ready to be consumed.
11. The application (IT App) consumes the messages from the queue immediately and starts processing the order.
12. When the order has been processed, the external application sends a message to the feedback queue (*receive*).

Receiving the confirmation

The process orders are periodically sent back to the ERP system for invoicing.

Trigger:

> The job scheduler triggers an event every 15 minutes.

Flow:

1. The job scheduler event starts a PL/SQL procedure, which processes the feedback message.
2. The message is consumed from the feedback queue (*receive*).
3. A SQL UPDATE command updates the status of the order in the ERP database.

Evaluation of the existing solution

By evaluating the existing solution we came to the following conclusions:

- This is an integration solution that has grown up over time using a wide variety of different technologies.
- A batch solution which does not support real-time integration. Exchanging information in files is not really a state-of-the-art solution.
- Exchanging information in files is not really a state-of-the-art solution.
    - Data cannot be exchanged reliably, as FTP does not support transactions.
    - Error handling and monitoring are difficult and time-consuming. (It's not easy to determine if the IT app does not send a response.)

- Files must be read and processed by the external applications, all of which use different methods.
- Integrating new distribution channels (such as web services) is difficult, as neither PL/SQL nor shell scripts are the ideal solution in this case.
- Many different technologies are used. The integration logic is distributed, which makes maintenance difficult:
  - Job scheduler (for orchestration)
  - PL/SQL (for orchestration and mediation)
  - Shell script (for orchestration and mediation)
- Different solutions are used for files and queues.

Many of these disadvantages are purely technical. From a business perspective, only the first disadvantage represents a real problem. The period of a maximum of 30 minutes between the data being entered in the ERP system, and the external systems being updated, is clearly too long. From a technical point of view, it is not possible to reduce this amount of time, as the batch solution overhead is significant and, in the case of shorter cycles, the total overhead would be too large.

Therefore, the decision was made to modernize the existing integration solution and to transform it into an event-driven, service-oriented integration solution based on the processing of individual orders.

Modernizing — integration with SOA

The main objective of the modernization process, from a business perspective, is the real-time integration of orders.

From a technical standpoint, there are other objectives, including the continued use of the batch mode through file connections. This means that the new solution must completely replace the old one, and the two solutions should not be left running in parallel. A further technical objective is that of improved support as a result of the introduction of a suitable infrastructure.

On the basis of these considerations, a new SOA-based integration architecture was proposed and implemented, as shown in the following diagram:

Chapter 4

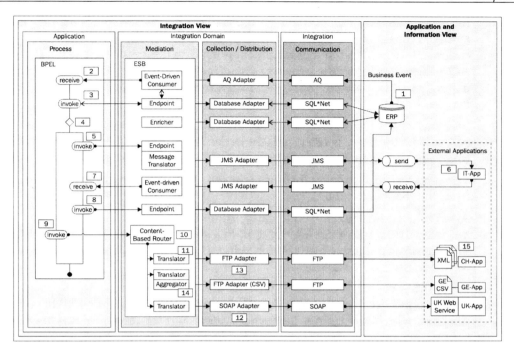

Trigger:

> Each new order is published to a queue in the ERP database, using the Change Data Capture functionality of the ERP system.

Flow:

1. The business event is consumed from the queue by an event-driven consumer building block in the ESB. The corresponding AQ adapter is used for this purpose.
2. A new BPEL process instance is started for the integration process. This instance is responsible for orchestrating all the integration tasks for each individual order.
3. First, the important order information concerning the products and the customer must be gathered, as the ERP system only sends the primary key for the new order in the business event. A service is called on the ESB that uses a database adapter to read the data directly from the ERP database, and compiles it into a message in canonical format.
4. A decision is made about the system to which the order should be sent, and about whether feedback on the order is expected.

5. In the right-hand branch, the message is placed in the existing output queue (*send*). A message translator building block converts the order from the canonical format, to the message format used so far, before it is sent. The AQ adapter supports the process of sending the message. The BPEL process instance will be paused until the callback from the external applications is received.
6. The message is processed by the external application in the same way as before. The message is retrieved, the order is processed, and, at a specified time, a feedback message is sent to the feedback queue (*receive*).
7. The paused BPEL process instance is reactivated and consumes the message from the feedback queue.
8. An invoke command is used to call another service on the ESB, which modifies the status of the ERP system in a similar way to the current solution. This involves a database adapter making direct modifications to a table or record in the ERP database.
9. In the other case, which is shown in the branch on the left, only a message is sent to the external systems. Another service is called on the ESB for this purpose, which determines the target system and the target format based on some information passed in the header of the message.
10. The ESB uses a header-based router to support the content-based forwarding of the message.
11. Depending on the target system, the information is converted from the canonical format to the correct target format.
12. The UK App already has a web service, which can be used to pass the order to the system. For this reason, this system is connected via an SOAP adapter.
13. The two other systems continue to use the file-based interface. Therefore, an FTP adapter creates and sends the files through FTP in XML or CSV format.
14. In order to ensure that the external application (labeled **GE App** in the diagram) still receives the information in batch mode, with several orders combined in one file, an aggregator building block is used. This collects the individual messages over a specific period of time, and then sends them together in the form of one large message to the target system via the FTP adapter.
15. An aggregation process is not needed for the interface to the other external application (labeled **CH App** in the image), as this system can also process a large number of small files.

Evaluation of the new solution

An evaluation of the new solution shows the following benefits:

- The orchestration is standardized and uses only one technology.
- One BPEL instance is responsible for one order throughout the entire integration process:
    - This simplifies the monitoring process, because the instance continues running until the order is completed; in other words, in one of the two cases until the feedback message from the external system has been processed.
- The orchestration is based only on the canonical format. The target system formats are generated at the last possible moment in the mediation layer:
    - Additional distribution channels can easily be added on the ESB, without having to modify the orchestration process.
    - The solution can easily support other protocols or formats that are not yet known, simply by adding an extra translator building block.

Trivadis Architecture Blueprints and integration

The Trivadis Architecture Blueprints (Liebhart et al. 2007) can be combined with the Integration Architecture Blueprint by incorporating the building blocks from the architecture blueprints into the integration blueprint.

Implementation scenarios

This is shown in the following diagram using the example of an architecture based on the Spring framework:

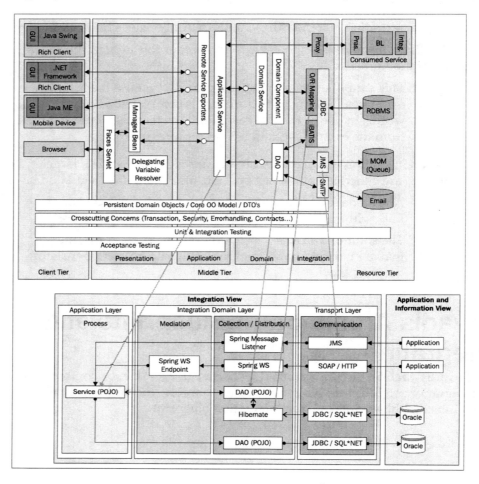

The (application) service is assigned to the process layer, as it is primarily responsible for orchestrating and managing the data accesses. As described in the **Spring Architecture Blueprint**, a data access from the service can use **Data Access Objects (DAOs)** with **Hibernate** or **Java Database Connectivity (JDBC)**. This corresponds to the building blocks made available by the Integration Architecture Blueprint. The service is used by two applications: One has a JMS connection using **Spring Message Listener** and the other a web service connection through **Spring Webservice Framework**.

As already described in *Chapter 3*, simple integration processes and steps can be combined to form more complex processes, by turning the target of one step in the process into the source for the next.

As shown in the following diagram, the **Microsoft .NET Architecture Blueprint** and the **Spring Architecture Blueprint** can be used to implement web services where the individual artifacts are assigned to the same layer. This is transparent for the integration blueprint, as these are simply applications which can be addressed using the appropriate protocol.

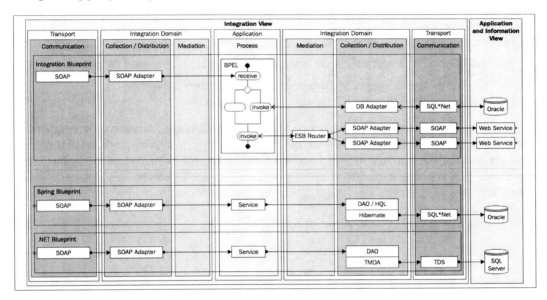

Applications based on the **Oracle ADF Architecture Blueprint** and **Oracle Forms Blueprint** can also be integrated in the same way.

Summary

You have now seen how the Trivadis Integration Architecture Blueprint can be used to illustrate integration scenarios that implement the various business patterns described in *Chapter 1*.

Most of the scenarios have been kept independent of specific vendor products on the integration level, and are based solely on the building blocks that form part of the different layers of the blueprint.

You should now be able to:

- Explain service-oriented integration scenarios
- Explain scenarios for implementing the business patterns for EAI/EII and data integration
- Understand the concept of modern integration scenarios using event processing business patterns, as well as grid computing and Extreme Transaction Processing (XTP)
- Explain how an ERP system (SAP) can be combined with the integration blueprint
- Explain how an existing integration solution can be updated using SOA, and describe a scenario that has already been implemented in practice
- Combine the integration blueprint with the other Trivadis Architecture Blueprints.

In the next chapter, we will map the products and platforms of some major vendors and of the open source community to the Trivadis Integration Architecture Blueprint. This should help you to see in which areas of the blueprint the vendors are active, and can guide you when comparing solutions of the different vendors.

5
Vendor Products for Implementing the Trivadis Blueprint

In this chapter, we will map not only single products, but complete product lines from a range of vendors to the Trivadis Integration Architecture Blueprint.

For implementing modern, **service-oriented integration architectures,** we will cover the following products and product lines:

- Oracle Fusion Middleware product line
- IBM WebSphere product line
- Microsoft Biztalk and .NET 3.0
- Spring framework combined with other open source software

For implementing more traditional, data integration architectures, we will cover the following products and product lines:

- Oracle Data Integration
- IBM Information Management
- Microsoft SQL Server Integration Services

Oracle Fusion Middleware product line

Oracle Fusion Middleware is a complete platform for designing, implementing and operating service-oriented integration architectures.

Vendor Products for Implementing the Trivadis Blueprint

The following diagram shows the Oracle Fusion Middleware components in the integration blueprint:

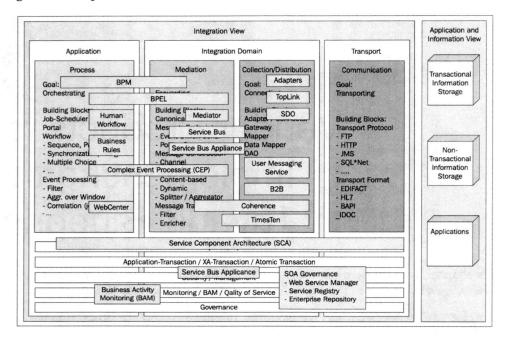

The following table holds a description of the components of the Oracle Fusion Middleware product line, as shown in this diagram:

Component	Description
Adapters	Oracle Adapters use **Java Connector Architecture (JCA)** technology to connect external systems to the Oracle SOA Suite.
	The Oracle SOA Suite includes out-of-the-box adapters to integrate with transport protocols, data stores, messaging middleware, and ERP systems, such as FTP, JMS, **Advanced Queuing (AQ)**, Websphere MQ, files, databases, Oracle applications, SAP, Siebel, and so on.
	Oracle offers other adapters under separate licenses that enable a wide range of systems and technologies, including SAP, Siebel, Tuxedo, CICS, and so on, to be integrated.
B2B	Oracle Integration B2B supports industry standard protocols, including **RosettaNet, Electronic Data Interchange (EDI), Applicability Statement 2 (AS2)**, and **UCCnet**, together with internal configurations. In addition, it provides out-of-the-box connectivity to industry hubs, such as Wal-Mart, Cisco, and Intel.

Component	Description
BPEL	The Oracle BPEL component offers a comprehensive and easy-to-use infrastructure for orchestrating, executing, monitoring, and improving business processes based on BPEL standards. BPEL processes can be executed.
BPM	The Oracle **Business Process Management** component is a complete set of tools for creating, executing, and optimizing business processes.
	The suite enables collaboration between Business and IT to automate and optimize business processes. The result is improved efficiency and agility, and lower costs.
	Oracle BPM is specially tuned for line-of-business users, and is based on the standard-based notation BPMN 2.0, which also allows for these processes to be executed.
BAM	Oracle **Business Activity Monitoring** provides business functionality for monitoring an organization's services and processes. KPIs are correlated down to the level of the business processes themselves, and BAM can be used to adapt the processes quickly and easily to changes in different circumstances.
	Oracle BAM is a complete solution for creating real-time, operational dashboards and for developing monitoring applications over the web.
Business Rules	The Oracle Business Rules component enables dynamic decisions to be made at runtime and allows the rules on which the decisions are based to be externalized, so that they can be adapted much more quickly and easily, sometimes even by business analysts themselves. This increase in agility is important, as it allows enterprises to remain competitive and to meet regulatory requirements.
Coherence	Oracle Coherence (formerly **Tangosol Coherence**) is a well known enterprise data grid implementation.
	It provides fast and reliable access to frequently used data, making it possible for organizations to scale mission-critical applications predictably. By automatically and dynamically partitioning data in memory across multiple servers, Coherence ensures continuous data availability and transactional integrity, even in the event of a server failure. Coherence is a shared infrastructure that combines data locality with local processing power to perform real-time data analyses, in-memory grid computations and parallel transaction, and event processing.

Component	Description
CEP	Oracle **Complex Event Processing** is a complete solution for building applications to filter, correlate, and process events in real time so that downstream applications, service-oriented architectures, and event-driven architectures are driven by true, real-time intelligence.
	Oracle CEP is an integral component of the SOA Suite that enables patterns in event streams to be identified by formulating corresponding queries. The CEP monitors these streams, stores the necessary individual and independent events, and attempts to correlate them into specific patterns. Users write the queries with the help of **Continuous Query Language (CQL)**.
Human Workflow	The Human Workflow component assigns a task, such as an order conformation, to a role or a user and waits until it receives a response. The user completes the task in a work-list application that displays current tasks and enables the user to process them individually.
Mediator	The Oracle Mediator component provides a lightweight framework to mediate between various components within a composite application in an SCA. Mediator converts data to facilitate communication between different interfaces exposed by different components, which are wired together to build an SOA composite application. Mediator facilitates integration between events and services, where service invocations and events can be mixed and matched. You can use a Mediator component to consume a business event or to receive a service invocation. A Mediator component can evaluate routing rules, perform transformations, validate, and either invoke another service or raise another business event.
OSB	**Oracle Service Bus** is a key component of the SOA Suite and the Event-driven Architecture Suite in the Oracle Fusion Middleware product family. OSB uniquely delivers the integration capabilities of an **Enterprise Service Bus (ESB)** with operational service management in a single product. OSB is designed to handle the deployment, management, and governance challenges of implementing service-oriented architecture (SOA) from department to enterprise scale. OSB is a proven, lightweight SOA integration platform designed for connecting, mediating, and managing interactions between heterogeneous services, and not just for web services, but also Java and .Net messaging services and legacy endpoints.

Component	Description
OSBA	The **Layer 7 Oracle Service Bus (L7 OSB) Appliance** combines the ESB capabilities of OSB with Layer 7's XML security to create a pre-integrated, pre-configured secure SOA integration solution that can reduce the cost and complexity of an SOA implementation. The OSB Appliance provides acceleration of CPU-intensive operations such as message parsing, data validation, and XML transformation, while the integral Layer 7 XML firewall provides DMZ-class threat protection, advanced identity integration, and message-level security capabilities to address the broadest range of external threats. By performing these tasks in a hardware appliance, OSBA ensures latency is reduced, applications aren't overloaded and service endpoints can offload computationally intensive operations to hardware.
SCA	The new Oracle middleware generation supports a service infrastructure based on the **Service Component Architecture** standard. The goal of SCA is to reduce IT complexity through a standardized framework for assembling disparate enterprise SOA components into a higher-level composite. SOA Suite 11*g* benefits greatly from SCA because it fundamentally simplifies the entire application lifecycle from development through deployment and management.
SDO	**Service Data Objects** specify a standard way to access data and can be used to modify business data regardless of how it is physically accessed. Developers and architects do not need to know the technical details of how to access a particular backend data source in order to use SDO in their composite applications. Consequently, they can use static or dynamic programming styles and obtain connected as well as disconnected access.
TimesTen	Oracle TimesTen In-Memory Database is a memory-optimized relational database that delivers very low response time and very high throughput for performance-critical systems. It is targeted to run in the application tier, close to applications, and optionally in process with applications. It can be used as the database of record or as a cache to the Oracle database. TimesTen databases fit entirely in physical memory. They are persistent and recoverable, and access to them is provided using standard SQL interfaces.
TopLink	TopLink is Oracle's object/relational (O/R) mapping tool (implementation of Data Mapper building block, see *Chapter 3, Integration Architecture Blueprint*) and, like Hibernate, offers a JPA-compliant interface (EJB 3). Java objects can be mapped to relational databases and to XML.

Vendor Products for Implementing the Trivadis Blueprint

Component	Description
User Messaging Service	Oracle User Messaging Service provides a general service that enables messages to be sent from applications to users through a range of different channels. It also routes incoming messages from devices to the correct applications.
	Messaging drivers implement transport protocols that send the messages along the different channels. The channels supported include e-mail, SMS, and **TTS** (**text to speech**).
WebCenter	WebCenter is a product that integrates enterprise services to form a standardized, context-sensitive web application. Using the Oracle WebCenter applications, developers can break down the boundaries between web-based portals and enterprise applications. As a result, they can rapidly create flexible, context-sensitive work environments that make use of rich, Ajax-based components, portlets, and content in an open, standards-based architecture.

Oracle Application Integration Architecture (AIA)

Oracle Application Integration Architecture (AIA) is a pre-built open architecture implementing the canonical data model pattern by so-called **Enterprise Business Objects (EBO)**. AIA is a collection of infrastructure components and tools packaged with methodology guidance for the purpose of creating loosely-coupled, standards-based integrations. AIA is designed as a service-oriented architecture with all of the interoperability features inherent in service-oriented designs. The concepts described above represent major components and capabilities of AIA, but not the specific terminology. AIA is based on several key components, which can be easily mapped into the Trivadis Integration Architecture Blueprint, as shown in the following diagram:

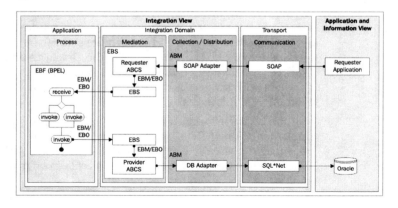

The following table holds a description of the components of the Application Integration Architecture (AIA).

Component	Description
ABCS	The role of the **Application Business Connector Service** is to expose the business functions provided by the participating application in a representation that conforms with **Enterprise Business Services** (EBSs). It also serves as a glue to allow the participating application to invoke the EBSs.
ABM	**Application Business Messages** are based on the application-specific terminology known and understood by those applications. These messages are translated into standard messages understood by AIA, specifically **Enterprise Business Messages** (EBM) used by EBSs.
CAVS	**Composite Application Validation System** provides a powerful end-to-end integration testing framework that allows an organization to develop all or part of an end-to-end test scenario, and simulate input and output from all applications involved in the integration flow.
EBF	**Enterprise Business Flows** represent business/integration processes that define and orchestrate a series of discrete steps to complete an integration task, such as synchronizing a product across multiple applications or submitting an order from CRM to the back office for fulfillment.
	EBFs are defined independently of the underlying applications, simplifying the process of integrating applications from multiple vendors. They will always use the services of the EBSs.
EBM	At the most basic level, **Enterprise Business Messages** are the messages that are exchanged between two applications. The EBM represents the specific content of an EBO needed for performing a specific activity.
EBO	The **Enterprise Business Object** is the definition for a standard business data object and is composed of reusable data components. The library of all EBOs makes up a data model. The EBO represents a layer of abstraction on top of the logical data model, and is targeted for use by developers, business users, and system integrators. In the integrations developed using AIA architecture, the EBO data model serves as a common data abstraction across systems. It supports the loose coupling of systems in AIA and eliminates the need for one-to-one mappings of the disparate data schemas between each set of systems.

Component	Description
EBS	**Enterprise Business Services** are the foundation blocks in the Oracle Application Integration Architecture. EBS represents the application-or implementation-independent web service definition for performing a business task. The architecture facilitates distributed processing using EBSs.
PIP	A **Process Integration Pack** is a pre-built set of integrated orchestration flows, application integration logic, and extensible enterprise business objects and services, required to manage the state and execution of a defined set of activities or tasks between specific Oracle applications associated with a given process.

Oracle Data Integrator

Oracle Data Integrator (ODI) is a product that streamlines the high performance movement and transformation of data between disparate systems in batch, real-time, synchronous, and asynchronous modes.

The **Extract, Load, and Transform** (ELT) architecture of the Oracle Data Integrator makes use of a wide range of **relational database management systems (RDBMS) engines**) to process and transform the data. This approach increases the performance and scalability of the system, and lowers the overall solution costs.

The Data Integrator is primarily intended for data integration tasks.

The following diagram shows the components of the ODI in the integration blueprint:

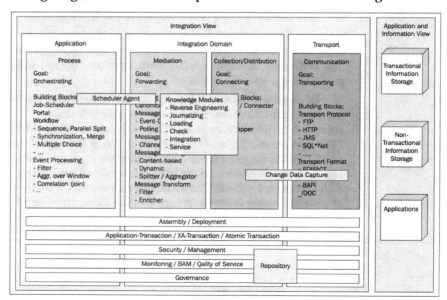

The following table holds a description of the components of the ODI:

Component	Description
KM	**Knowledge Modules** implement the actual data flows and define the templates for generating code across the multiple systems involved in each process. The modules are generic, because they allow data flows to be generated regardless of the transformation rules. However, they are also highly specific, because the code they generate and the integration strategy they implement are finely tuned for a given technology. ODI provides a comprehensive library of Knowledge Modules: • **Reverse Engineering KM**: This module is used for reading the data from tables and other objects in source databases. • **Journalizing KM**: This module is used to record in a journal the new and changed data within either a table or view. It implements **Change Data Capture** (**CDC**) functionality. • **Loading KM**: This module is used for efficient extraction of data from source databases and includes database-specific utilities, such as bulk unload. • **Integration KM**: This module is used to load data into the target database. • **Check KM**: This ensures that constraints in the source and target databases are not violated. • **Service KM**: This module provides the capability to make data services (data as web services) available.
Repository	The Repository stores information about models and projects, together with runtime information. It is used by the Designer and the Scheduler Agents. All the objects configured and used by the Data Integrator modules are stored in the Repository.
Scheduler Agent	The Scheduler Agent coordinates the execution of integration processes. It can be installed on any platform that supports a **Java Virtual Machine** (**JVM**). The execution can be started by the integral scheduler or an external, third-party scheduler.

IBM WebSphere product line

WebSphere is a product line developed by IBM that includes a range of software products for application integration, an infrastructure, and an integrated development environment.

The following diagram shows the IBM WebSphere components in the integration blueprint:

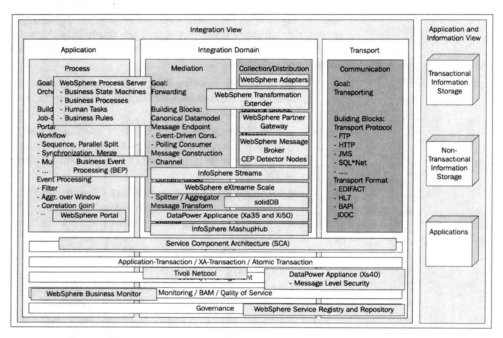

The following table holds a description of the components of the IBM WebSphere product line, as shown in this diagram:

Component	Description
BEP	**Business Event Processing** refers to the capability of monitoring message processing in a business context.
	Business Event Processing enables business units to define, design, and create business events and behavior patterns without the involvement of the IT department or additional programming. The product provides graphical tools for bi-directional monitoring and visualization of all activity flows. Patterns, rather than static rules, form the basis of the product, providing users with comprehensive functionality for creating actions based on individual messages and events, or combinations of the two.

Component	Description
DataPower Appliance	IBM's SOA DataPower Appliances are purpose-built, easy-to-deploy network devices to simplify, help secure and accelerate XML and web services deployments, and, at the same time, to extend the SOA infrastructure. These devices allow an innovative, pragmatic approach to be taken to the implementation of service-oriented architecture, while also protecting existing investments in applications, security, and network infrastructure. The following devices are available: • **XI50**: This device offers transport-independent transformations between binary files, flat-text files, and XML messages for secure XML enablement, enterprise message buses, and mainframe connectivity. • **XA35**: This device can speed up common types of XML processing by offloading them from servers and networks. It can perform XML parsing, XML schema validation, XML Path Language (XPath) routing, Extensible Stylesheet Language Transformations (XSLT), XML compression, and other essential XML processing with wirespeed XML performance. • **XS40**: This device guarantees the security of XML messages and web services transactions, including encryption, firewall filtering, digital signatures, schema validation, WS-Security, XML access control, XPath, and detailed logging.
InfoSphere MashupHub	InfoSphere MashupHub is a light-weight information management environment for IT and business professionals who wish to publish and share web, departmental, personal, and enterprise information for use in Web 2.0 applications and mashups. MashupHub includes visual tools for creating, storing, transforming, and remixing feeds to be used in mashup and situational applications. It also includes a central catalog for users to tag, rate, and share "mashable" assets.
InfoSphere Streams	InfoSphere Streams provides an execution platform and services for user-developed applications that ingest, filter, analyze, and correlate potentially massive volumes of continuous data streams. It supports the composition of new applications in the form of stream processing graphs that can be created on the fly, mapped to a variety of hardware configurations, and adapted as requests come and go. InfoSphere Streams is comparable to Oracle CEP and Microsoft's StreamInsight.

Vendor Products for Implementing the Trivadis Blueprint

Component	Description
solidDB	IBM solidDB product family features relational, in-memory database technology that delivers better performance, performing up to ten times faster than conventional, disk-based databases. solidDB uses the familiar SQL language to access the data.
Tivoli Netcool	Tivoli Netcool strengthens the Tivoli portfolio to help enterprises, service providers, and government agencies manage the critical services they deliver to customers and end users across complex technology infrastructures. Netcool supports IBM Service Management, a comprehensive, modular approach to integrated service visibility and control.
WebSphere Adapters	WebSphere Adapters use **Java Connector Architecture (JCA)** technology to connect external systems to the process server, ESB, or Message Broker. The adapters can integrate with different transport protocols, data stores, messaging middleware, and ERP systems, such as FTP, JMS, Websphere MQ, files, databases, Oracle applications, SAP, Siebel, and so on.
WebSphere Business Monitor	IBM WebSphere Business Monitor is a comprehensive **Business Activity Monitoring (BAM)** software product that provides an up-to-date view of an organization's business performance. Customizable business dashboards process business events and data and calculate **Key Performance Indicators (KPIs)** and metrics. The events and data can be collected from a wide variety of sources, including WebSphere Process Server and IBM FileNet P8 BPM. Adapters can be used to access data from other sources.
WebSphere Enterprise Service Bus	IBM WebSphere Enterprise Service Bus offers a standards-based integration platform for the easy connection of services. Web services connectivity, messaging with **Java Message Service (JMS)**, and service-oriented integration increase flexibility and keep downtimes to a minimum. An ESB executes the integration logic and allows for intelligent interaction between business events and endpoints.
WebSphere eXtreme Scale	IBM WebSphere eXtreme Scale is the IBM in-memory data-grid product. It can be described as a fully elastic, memory-based storage grid. It virtualizes the free memory of a potentially large number of Java virtual machines, and makes them behave like a single key-addressable storage pool for application states. Applications can view this as a network-attached storage medium. It is key addressable and applications can store a value at a key. Data within the grid can be replicated to achieve fault tolerance and protect against data loss. IBM WebSphere eXtreme Scale is comparable to Oracle coherence.

Component	Description
WebSphere Message Broker	WebSphere Message Broker can act as a message and protocol switch, enabling disparate applications and business data to be connected across multiple platforms, and providing functions for implementing an intelligent routing of an organization's entire business data. Business data can be made available in the required format exactly where it is needed.
WebSphere Message Broker CEP Detector Nodes	This is an extension of the Message Broker with **Complex Event Processing (CEP)** functionality.
WebSphere Partner Gateway	The Partner Gateway provides centralized and consolidated B2B trading partner and transaction management, to enable and manage process and data integration with trading partners.
	It is useful for companies that need a single point of management for all B2B trading-partner integration and that need to support a wide range of B2B transport protocols, such as **Electronic Data Interchange over the Internet (EDIINT)** AS1, AS2, and AS3; commerce XML (cXML); RosettaNet Implementation Framework (RNIF), Version 1.1 and 2.0; and e-business XML Messaging Service (ebMS), Version 2.0, as well as industry data formats (for example, EDI) and industry XML implementations. It combines comprehensive trading partner and transaction management capabilities, with support for a wide range of standards-based transport protocols and industry data formats to provide data exchange, process integration, and web services interoperability among trading partners.
WebSphere Portal	The IBM WebSphere Portal adapts to users' needs and delivers a composite view that allows the user to interact with several backend systems, as if there were only one system in use.
WebSphere Process Server	The WebSphere Process Server provides a runtime environment for business processes and acts as a process integration platform for business services on the basis of an SOA. It consists of the following components: • **Business State Machines**: supports the modeling of business processes as a sequence of states and events. • **Business Processes:** implements a BPEL-compliant process engine. BPEL models can be created in WebSphere Integration Developer or imported from a business model that has been produced in WebSphere Business Modeler. • **Human Tasks**: standardized components that can be used to assign activities to end users. • **Business Rules**: enables business rules to be externalized from the business process and increases their flexibility by allowing them to be adapted more rapidly.

Vendor Products for Implementing the Trivadis Blueprint

Component	Description
WebSphere Service Registry and Repository	This product improves the management and governance of services. Through its robust registry and repository capabilities and its close integration with IBM SOA Foundation, WebSphere Service Registry and Repository can be an essential base component of an SOA implementation.
	The WebSphere Service Registry and Repository system allows information about the services in an SOA, commonly referred to as service metadata, to be stored, accessed, and managed, in order to support a successful SOA implementation.
WebSphere TX	WebSphere **Transformation Extender (TX)** is a universal data transformation and validation engine. It tackles one of the major challenges of integrating enterprise systems, in other words, the processing of complex data. WebSphere TX can convert and assess the content of high volumes of large, multipart documents with complex formatting, using a codeless, graphical approach to development.

IBM Information Management software

IBM Information Management software allows data to be stored, accessed, and analyzed in a wide range of environments.

The products from the IBM Information Management software portfolio are primarily focused on data integration.

The following diagram shows the IBM Information Management software components in the integration blueprint:

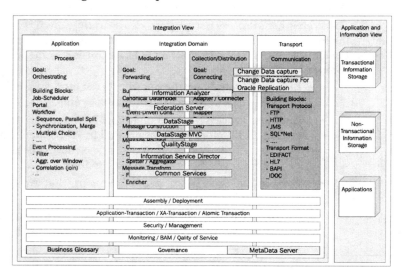

The following table holds a description of the components of IBM Information Management software, as shown in the preceding diagram:

Component	Description
Business Glossary	The Business Glossary helps organizations to create and manage a controlled vocabulary that acts as the common language between Business and IT. This is an important step towards aligning technology more effectively with business goals.
Change Data Capture	This is a real-time Change Data Capture and replication solution for heterogeneous environments. It identifies and distributes information within diverse data stores in realtime.
Change Data Capture for Oracle Replication	IBM InfoSphere Change Data Capture for Oracle Replication distributes data in realtime within Oracle systems.
DataStage	DataStage enables organizations to design data flows that can be used to extract information from different source systems. This information can be enriched by means of transformations, and is ultimately supplied to one or more target databases or applications (supports ETL processing).
DataStage MVS Edition	DataStage MVS Edition brings data transformation to IBM mainframes. It consolidates, collects, and centralizes information from several systems and mainframes.
Federation Server	Federation Server gives virtual access to enterprise information, as if it came from a single source, and, at the same time, preserves the integrity of the sources in question. The solution has transparent access to data from disparate sources, including relational, structured, and unstructured data, XML files, messages, and web services.
Information Analyzer	IBM WebSphere Information Analyzer helps to give an understanding of the structure, content, and quality of data sources. It allows a profile to be created for source systems, gives an insight into the systems themselves and monitors data rules.
Information Service Director	Information Service Director enables transformation, federation, and data-quality testing functionality to be published as a service within an SOA. As a result, developers can quickly and easily provide a service consisting of data integration logic that has been developed using the Information Server.
Metadata Server	The Metadata Server provides a metadata repository that is integrated with all the product modules in the Information Server. The metadata infrastructure is designed in such a way that the metadata can be managed more easily, and be used within one SOA by disparate technologies.

Component	Description
QualityStage	This module is responsible for a range of data cleansing and standardization tasks. Users can adapt and correct data (such as addresses or e-mail addresses) using the rules provided. These rules can also be extended. For example, when consolidating customer data it is possible to search for duplicates in the standardized records. The duplicates can be removed or combined if they are incomplete.

Microsoft BizTalk and .NET 3.0

BizTalk Server is the Microsoft server for **Business Process Management (BPM)**, **integration (EAI)**, and **service-oriented architectures (SOA)**. Business processes can be mapped, defined, executed, and analyzed within the IT environment using BizTalk server.

.NET is the Microsoft development platform. Since version 3.0, the .NET framework has included additional functionality relating to integration architectures, such as **Windows Communication Foundation (WCF)**, **Windows Workflow Foundation (WF)**, or the identity system **CardSpace**.

The following diagram shows the Microsoft BizTalk and .NET components in the integration blueprint:

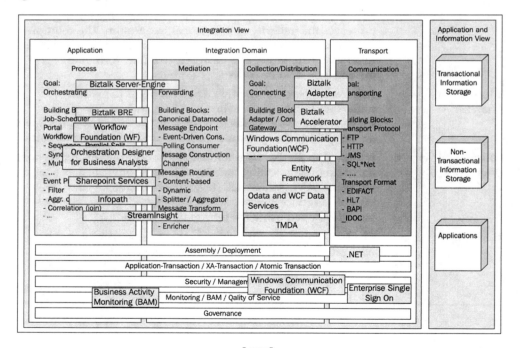

The following table holds a description of the components of Microsoft BizTalk and other server products, as shown in the preceding diagram:

Component	Description
BizTalk Accelerators	BizTalk Server Accelerators speed up the implementation of solutions. Microsoft provides accelerators for SWIFT and RosettaNet among others.
BizTalk Adapters	Because BizTalk Server needs to communicate with a variety of other software, it relies on the BizTalk Adapters to make this possible. An adapter is an implementation of a communication mechanism, such as a particular protocol. All the adapters are built on a standard base called the **Adapter Framework**. BizTalk server is supplied with more than 20 adapters. These include adapters for BASE EDI (EDIFACT and X.12), files, FTP, HTTP, MSMQ/MSMQT, POP3, SMTP, SOAP, Websphere MQ, SharePoint Services, WSE, SQL Server, Oracle Database, TIBCO, SAP R/3 (Version 4.x and 6.20), Siebel, and PeopleSoft. If other adapters are needed, they can be developed individually or acquired from third-party suppliers.
BRE	The **BizTalk Rules Engine** enables the creation of policies consisting of individual rules. The BRE can evaluate documents on the basis of specified rules, and apply the actions defined in the rules to the documents. The policies can be called from orchestrations. However, policies can also be used by any application that the BRE has an appropriate API for.
BizTalk Server Engine	The BizTalk Server Engine is the heart of the product. It consists of two main components: - A *messaging* component that provides the ability to communicate with a range of other software. By relying on exchangeable adapters for different kinds of communication, the BizTalk Server Engine can support a variety of protocols and data formats. - Support for creating and running graphically-defined processes called *orchestrations*. Built on top of the BizTalk Server Engine's messaging components, orchestrations implement the logic that drives all or part of a business process.

Component	Description
Business Activity Monitoring	BizTalk makes it possible to implement business processes by connecting several systems together. The users of these business processes need to be able to find out the status of the processes. In order to provide users with an accurate picture of the current status of one or more processes, the Business Activity Monitoring modules collect permanent data from running processes, and store it in a database.
Infopath	Infopath is a Windows application program that enables XML-based forms to be designed and filled with information. The proprietary, XML-based file format of the Infopath files takes a similar approach to the W3C XForms standard to represent form fields and control elements of data instances in XML format.
	The main target group consists of organizations with homogeneous work environments that need to be able to integrate forms into workflows.
Orchestration Designer for Business Analysts	Orchestration Designer for Business Analyst is a tool that enables business analysts to create orchestration data flows in the familiar Microsoft Visio environment. The complex flows can then be exported to the orchestration designer and used by developers to implement the orchestrations.
SharePoint Server	**Microsoft Office SharePoint Server (MOSS)** is an extension of **Windows SharePoint Services (WSS)**.
	Among other things, it offers more features for workflows, business intelligence, searches, and managing large web sites.
SharePoint Services	The purpose of WSSs is to optimize the cooperation between users within one web user interface. The fundamental structure of Windows SharePoint Services ensures that the cooperation between the people involved is integrative and subject based.
	WSS is a free add-on to Windows Server and includes templates for creating document libraries, blogs, wikis, and meeting workspaces.
	WSS also offers a workflow environment, which enables the publishing process for a document, or the authorization of vacation requests, for example, to be represented (support for human workflows).

Component	Description
StreamInsight	Microsoft StreamInsight is a solution for building applications to filter, correlate, and process events in real-time so that downstream applications, service-oriented architectures, and event-driven architectures are driven by true, real-time intelligence.
	StreamInsight was planned to be a part of the Microsoft SQL Server product, but it is technically independent. StreamInsight has a .NET-based API. Developers implement input and output adapters as .NET classes that can connect to any kind of data producers or consumers of event streams. Filtering, aggregation, and correlation of event streams are formulated LINQ queries that are run by the StreamInsight engine.

The following table holds a description of the components of Microsoft .NET 3.0 and 3.5:

Component	Description
Enterprise Single Sign On	When systems from different manufacturers are integrated, the user names and passwords that allow access to these systems must be made available. On the one hand, the information must be treated as strictly confidential (encrypted storage), while on the other hand, a mechanism is needed to assign Windows accounts to user accounts on backend systems.
	From version 3.0 of .NET onwards, Microsoft has supplied CardSpace, a token-based identity metasystem, which uses standardized WS-* protocols, such as WS-Security, WS-Trust, WS-MetadataExchange, and WS-SecurityPolicy. CardSpace can be integrated with any product that supports these protocols.
Entity Framework	The Entity Framework is Microsoft's O/R mapper, which was introduced together with SQL Server 2008. Entity Framework maps database and domain models using XML files.
	The Entity Framework offers an open provider model, and database manufacturers such as IBM and Oracle have already announced their own providers.
	It works as an LINQ provider that allows .NET developers to formulate queries in the **Language integrated Query (LINQ)** syntax that has been introduced with .NET version 3.5.

Component	Description
OData and WCF Data Services	The **Open Data Protocol** (**OData**) is a highly interoperable "RESTful" Web protocol for querying and updating data. OData builds upon Web technologies such as HTTP, **Atom Publishing Protocol** (**AtomPub**), and JSON. OData is released under Microsoft's *Open Specification Promise* that allows anyone to freely use and implement OData.
	WCF Data Services allow for an easy implementation of an OData data service based on .NET (3.5 SP1 and 4.0) and the Entity Framework.
	With IBM's **WebSphere eXtreme Scale REST** data service, there is already a non-Microsoft implementation of OData.
Trivadis TMDA	**Trivadis Managed Data Access** is a generator, that enables a data access layer with the accompanying dataset and filter classes to be created on the basis of an existing database schema and configuration file. However, TMDA also has a class library (the actual data access layer) that provides powerful functions for programming database accesses.
WCF	**Windows Communication Foundation** combines the remoting, **Microsoft Message Queues** (**MSMQ**), DCOM, and web services communications technologies within one newly developed, standardized API. It also incorporates additional web services protocols, such as WS-Security and WS-Transactions, which previously had to be installed separately as **Web Services Enhancements** (**WSE**). In addition, WCF integrates distributed transactions with COM+.
	The philosophy behind WCF is frequently summarized as *ABC* or *address*, *binding*, and *contract*.
WF	**Workflow Foundation** is the workflow engine of BizTalk. It enables sequential or state-driven workflows to be defined, and business rules to be tested. In this case, the implementation of the rule manager is equivalent to the instantiation of the policy activity of Workflow Foundation. Windows Workflow Foundation (WF) is part of .NET 3.0.

Microsoft SQL Server Integration Services

Microsoft SQL Server Integration Services (**SSIS**) is a comprehensive data integration platform that is used to transport, call, transform, and consolidate information from disparate sources and to upload it to several different systems. It is the successor to **Data Transformation Services** (**DTS**).

Chapter 5

The SSIS is primarily intended for data integration tasks.

The following diagram shows the components of Microsoft SQL Server Integration Services in the integration blueprint:

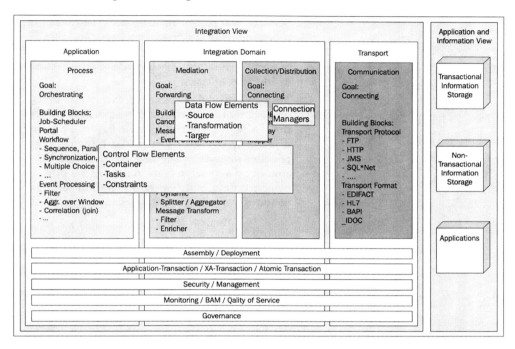

The following table holds a description of the components of SQL Server Integration Services, as shown in the preceding diagram:

Component	Description
Connection Managers	A Connection Manager is a logical representation of a connection.
	SQL Server Integration Services provides a variety of different connection managers that packages can use to create connections with a range of data sources and servers.
	The following connection types are supported, among others: ADO, ADO.NET, Excel, file, flat file, FTP, HTTP, MSMQ, MSOLAP, OLEDB, ODBC, and SMTP.

Component	Description

Control Flow Elements	SQL Server Integration Services provides three different types of Control Flow Elements:
	
	- **Containers**: Objects in SQL Server Integration Services that provide a structure. They support repeating control flows in packages and they group tasks and containers into meaningful units of work. Containers can include other containers in addition to tasks.
	- **Tasks**: Control flow elements that define units of work that are performed in a package control flow. A SQL Server Integration Services package is made up of one or more tasks. If the package contains more than one task, the tasks are connected and sequenced in the control flow by constraints. SQL Server Integration Services includes the following types of tasks:
	  - Data flow tasks
	  - Data preparation tasks
	  - Workflow tasks
	  - SQL server tasks
	  - Scripting tasks
	  - Analysis service tasks
	  - Maintenance tasks
	- **Precedence constraints**: Constraints connect executables, containers, and tasks to form an ordered control flow.

Data Flow Elements	SQL Server Integration Services provides three different types of Data Flow components: - **Sources**: This component extracts data from data stores, such as tables and views in relational databases, files, and SQL Server Analysis Services databases. - **Transformations**: This component modifies, summarizes, and cleans data. - **Destinations**: This component loads data into data stores or creates in-memory datasets.

Spring framework combined with other open source software

The Spring framework is an open source framework for the Java platform. The purpose of the Spring framework (often referred to simply as *Spring*) is to simplify development with Java/JavaEE and to promote good programming practice. Spring has a wide range of functionality and offers an end-to-end solution for developing applications and business logic. The focus is on decoupling individual framework components and on the interaction of a variety of platforms and tools, ranging from J2EE servers and persistence tools, to web integration.

The Spring Integration and Spring Batch subprojects, and other components in the open source environment that can easily be combined with the Spring Universe, enable the Spring framework to be used for integration solutions.

The following diagram shows the components of the Spring framework and other open source software in the integration blueprint:

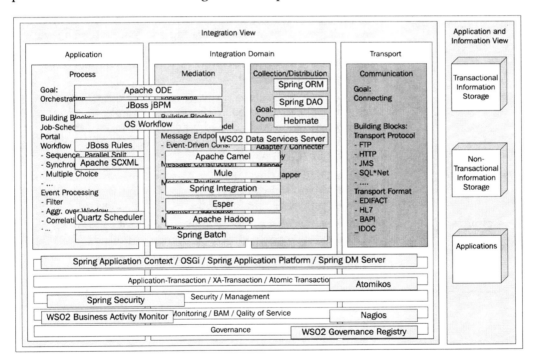

The following table holds a description of the components of the Spring framework and other open source software, as shown in the preceding diagram:

Component	Description
Apache Camel	Apache Camel is a powerful open source integration framework, which supports and implements most of the patterns/building blocks described in *Chapter 2, Base Technologies*. Camel allows for the creation of the Enterprise Integration Patterns to implement routing and mediation rules in either a Java-based domain-specific language (or Fluent API), through Spring-based XML Configuration files, or through the **Scala DSL**.
Apache Commons SCXML	**State Chart XML (SCXML)** is currently a Working Draft published by the World Wide Web Consortium (W3C). SCXML provides a generic state-machine-based execution environment based on Harel State Tables.
	Apache Commons SCXML is a candidate for the control language within multiple markup languages coming out of the W3C (see Working Draft for details). *Commons SCXML* is an implementation aimed at creating and maintaining a Java SCXML engine that is capable of executing a state machine defined using a SCXML document, while abstracting out the environment interfaces.
Apache Hadoop	Apache Hadoop is a Java software framework that supports data-intensive distributed applications. It enables applications to work with thousands of nodes and petabytes of data. Hadoop was inspired by Google's MapReduce and **Google File System** (**GFS**) papers.
Apache ODE	Apache ODE was developed by Apache Software Foundation and stands for **Orchestration Director Engine**. It can execute business processes that follow the WS-BPEL standard.
Atomikos	Atomikos provides a transaction management solution for XTP, SOA, and open source environments offering basic support for JDBC/XA pools, JMS/XA pools, and JTA/XA to enable functional testing of transaction processes outside of the application server.

Component	Description
Esper	Esper is an open source event processor for CEP and ESP applications. Esper simplifies and speeds up the development of applications with a large number of incoming events or messages. This enables events to be analyzed, filtered, and consumed in different ways, and in real time.
	Because it is a pure CEP engine, Esper must be embedded in an application in such a way that the events can be passed to the engine, and the corresponding actions carried out. Therefore, Esper is also ideally suited to integration in the Spring platform.
	Esper has its own query language called **Event Processing Language** (**EPL**), which has many similarities with SQL.
Hibernate	Hibernate is an open source persistence framework for Java. The framework allows the status of an object in a relational database to be stored, and objects to be created from the corresponding records. This functionality is referred to as **Object-Relational Mapping** (**ORM**), and it means that developers do not need to program SQL queries. It ensures that the application is independent of the SQL dialect of the database. The objects are standard objects with attributes and methods (referred to in Java as POJOs, or plain old Java objects). The relationships between the objects are mapped to the corresponding database relationships.
JBoss Rules	JBoss Rules is an open source rule engine. It takes the form of a library and is available free of charge with an Apache license. At the heart of the rule engine is an inference engine. Its job is to match facts and rules (pattern matching) in order to make conclusions that trigger corresponding actions.
jBPM	jBPM is a framework developed by JBoss for the purpose of implementing workflows for the Java EE platform. The **Java Process Definition Language** (**jPDL**) is used to define the processes. The jPDL is a format based on XML that is only used in the jBPM. A graphical editor is also available for the jPDL.
Mule	Mule is a set of components that allows independent applications to communicate with one other simply (often in a purely declarative form) through a virtualized transport layer. In principle, Mule is an implementation of the Enterprise Integration Patterns, presented in (Hohpe, Wolf 2004).
Nagios	Nagios is a popular open source computer system and network-monitoring software application. It watches hosts and services, alerting users when things go wrong, and again when the errors have been fixed.

Vendor Products for Implementing the Trivadis Blueprint

Component	Description
OS Workflow	OS Workflow from OpenSymphony is a basic implementation of a workflow engine, which is highly flexible. It uses its own dialect of XML to describe the workflows, and a rudimentary GUI editor is available for the XML dialect.
OSGi	The specification of the **Open Service Gateway initiative** service platform is a Java-based runtime environment above the level of JVMs and their basic services. One of the main features of the service platform is its ability to execute dynamic, controlled service applications (referred to as bundles) at runtime and, most importantly, to update and then remove them. The model of the OSGi service platform therefore makes it possible to run different, largely independent, modular applications in parallel on the same virtual machine, and to manage and update them remotely throughout the entire lifecycle of the applications. Dependencies between bundles are automatically resolved and an intelligent version management system is available.
Quartz Scheduler	Quartz Scheduler is an open source job scheduling system that can be integrated with any J2EE or J2SE application, or used as a standalone solution. Quartz can be used to create simple or complex workflow plans with just a few hundred or several thousand jobs, where a job is a standard component such as an EJB or a **Spring bean** (**POJO**). Quartz supports distributed transactions and clustering.
Spring Batch	Spring Batch is a light-weight, comprehensive batch framework designed to enable the development of robust batch applications that are vital for the daily operations of enterprise systems.
	Spring Batch provides reusable functions that are essential in processing large volumes of records, including logging/tracing, transaction management, job processing statistics, job restart, skip, and resource management. It also provides technical services that enable extremely high-volume and high-performance batch jobs to be created through the use of optimization and partitioning techniques.
Spring Integration	Spring Integration provides an extension of the Spring programming model to support the well-known Enterprise Integration Patterns (Hohpe, Wolf 2004), while building on the Spring Framework's existing integration mechanisms.
	It enables messaging within Spring-based applications and integrates with external systems through adapters. These adapters provide a higher level of abstraction than the Spring framework support for remoting, messaging, and scheduling.

Component	Description
Spring ORM and DAO	The Spring ORM module is an integration of the most popular ORM framework. However, it does not provide its own ORM solution, but instead integrates Hibernate, Oracle TopLink, JDO, and iBATIS SQL Maps in a standardized form.
	The Spring DAO module is an abstraction of JDBC, which significantly simplifies programming for the JDBC API.
Spring Security	Spring Security provides comprehensive security services for J2EE-based enterprise software applications. There is a particular emphasis on supporting projects built using The Spring framework, which is the leading J2EE solution for enterprise software development. If you're not using Spring for developing enterprise applications, we warmly encourage you to take a closer look at it. Some familiarity with Spring—and in particular, dependency injection principles—will help you get up to speed with Spring Security more easily.
SpringSource Application Platform	The SpringSource Application Platform is a completely modular Java application server designed to run enterprise Java applications and Spring-powered applications. The platform is based on the new SpringSource Dynamic Module Kernel, and provides a module-based server, which uses the power of Spring, Apache Tomcat, and OSGi.
WSO2 BAM	The **WSO2 Business Activity Monitor** serves the needs of both business and IT domain experts to monitor and understand business activities within an SOA deployment. While specifically designed to monitor SOA deployments, it can be extended to cater to other general monitoring requirements as well.
	WSO2 BAM supports both **zero latency**, as well as **straight through processing**. Data is collected through push or pull models, automatically, and processed in real time, to be made available for business and IT users.
WSO2 Data Services Server	The WSO2 Data Services Server augments SOA development efforts by providing an easy-use platform for creating and hosting data services. Data services are essentially web services that provide unprecedented access to data stored in heterogeneous data stores, thus enabling easy integration of data into business processes, mashups, gadgets, BI applications, and any service in general.

Component	Description
WSO2 Governance Registry	WSO2 Governance Registry addresses both design-time and runtime governance scenarios, to ensure compliance with corporate standards. It allows enterprise architects and developers to always keep track of the services being created and used within an SOA. The WSO2 Governance Registry connects SOA infrastructure with the people, processes, and policies essential to an effective SOA.

Summary

In this chapter, you have seen how various products and product lines from a range of vendors can be mapped to the Trivadis Integration Architecture Blueprint.

By now you should know which products from each vendor can be used for implementing modern service-oriented integration architectures, as well as more traditional data integration architectures.

With this knowledge and the architectural guidelines, you should now be able to successfully implement your own integration projects.

References

(Adams et Al. 2001)   *J. Adams, S. Koushik, G. Vasudeva, G. Galambos:* Patterns for e-business, IBM Press, August 2001

(Ambriola, Tortora 1993)   *V. Ambriola, G. Tortora:* Advances in Software Engineering and Knowledge Engineering, World Scientific Publishing Company, December 1993

(Andrews et al. 2003)   *T. Andrews, F. Curbera, H. Dholakia, Y. Goland, J. Klein, F. Leymann, K. Liu, D. Roller, D. SMith, S. Thattte, I. Trickovic, S. Weerawarana:* Business Process Execution Language for Web Services, OASIS 5.5.2003

(Alves et al. 2006)   *A. Alves, A. Arkin, S. Askary, B. Bloch F. Curbera, Y. Goland, N. Kartha, , C. Kevin, V. Mehta, S. Thatte, D. Vander Rijn, P. Yendluri, A. Yui:* Web Services Business Process Execution Language Version 2.0, OASIS Committee Draft, 17th May, 2006

(Beatty et al. 2003)   *J. Beatty, S. Brodsky, M. Nally, R. Patel:* Next-Generation Data Programming: Service Data objects, A Joint Whitepaper with IBM and BEA, November 2003

(Barber, Edwards 2007)   *G. Barber, M. Edwards:* Service Data Objects Specifications, Open Service Oriented Architecture, 2007

(Berenson et al. 95)   *H. Berenson, P. Bernstein, G. Gray, J. Melton, E. O'Neil, P. O'Neil:* A Critique of ANSI SQL Isolation Levels, Proceedings of the ACM SIGMOD Conference, San Jose, 1995

(Bernus et al. 2003)   *P. Bernus, L. Nemes, G. Schmidt:* Handbook on Enterprise Architecture International Handbooks on Information Systems, Springer, November 2003

(BrichHanson 1970)   *P. BrinchHanson:* The Nucleus of a Multiprogramming System, Communications of the ACM, April 1970

References

(Brunner 2007)   L. Brunner: Delivering the Goods, The Seybold Report Volume 7 Number 8 2007

(Carter 2007)   S. Carter: SOA & Web 2.0 — The New Language of Business, Pearson, 2007

(Casanave 2007)   C. Casanave: Designing a Semantic Repository — Integrating architecures for reuse and integration, ModelDriven.org 2007

(Chappell 2004)   D.A. Chappell: Enterprise Service Bus, O'Reilly, 2004

(Coral8 2007)   Coral8 Inc.: Complex Event Processing: Ten Design Patterns, 2007

(Craggs 2003)   S. Craggs: Best-of-Breed ESB, EAI Consortium, June 2003

(CSSWIFT 2005)   Credit Suisse, Bank Leu, Bank Hofmann: Private Swift Network (PSN) for EAM, User Procedure Manual, Credit Suisse Group 2005

(Damodaran 2004)   S. Damodaran: B2B integration over the Internet with XML: RosettaNet successes and challenges, International World Wide Web Conference ACM 2004

(Edwards 2007)   M. Edwards: Service Component Architecture (SCA), OASIS 2007

(Eugster et al. 2003)   P. Th. Eugster, P. A. Felber, R. Guerraoui, A-M. Kermarrec: The Many Faces of Pubish/Subscribe, ACM Computing Surveys, June 2003

(FIPS 1993)   Federal Information Processing Standards Publication 161-1: Electronic Data Interchange (EDI), April 1993

(Foster, Kesselmann 1999)   I. Foster, C. Kesselmann: The Grid — Blueprint of a New Computing Infrastructure (Morgan Kaufmann Publishers, San Francisco 1999)

(Fröschle, Reinheimer 2007)   H-P. Fröschle St. Reinheimer (Hrsg): Service-Oriented Architecture (SOA), HMD Heft 253, dpunkt Verlag, 2007

(Gartner 2006)   Gartner Group: Technology Hype cycle 2006, Gartner, 07/2006

(Gilfix 2003)   M. Gilfix: Managing Evolution of Integration Middleware via Integration Architecture Design, IBM 2003

(Gorton 2006)   I. Gorton: Essential Software Architecture, Springer 2006

(Grangard et al. 2001)   A. Grangard, B. Eisenberg, D. Nikull: ebXML Technical Architecture Specification v1.0.4, OASIS, February 2001

(Gray, Reuter 1993)   J. Gray, A. Reuter: Transaction Processing: Concepts and Techniques, Morgan Kaufmann; First edition, 1993

(Gruber et al. 2005)   O. Gruber, B-J. Hargrave, J. McAffer, P.Rapicault, T. Watson: The Eclipse 3.0 platform: Adopting OSGi technology, IBM Systems Journal 2005, VOL 44, NO. 2

(Haiduk et al. 2002)   P. Haiduk, P. Heusinger, M. Wagner: Use of OSGi on hardware-limitted components, Fraunhofer Institute for Integrated Circuits, Nürnberg 2002

(Hall et al. 2005)   J. Hall, K.A. Healy, R. G. Ross, R.,G.: The Business Motivation Model – Business Governance in a Volatile World, The Business Rules Group, Release 1.2 , September 2005

(Hapner et al. 2002)   M. Hapner, R. Burridge,R. Sharma ,J. Fialli, L. Stout: Java Message Service, Version 1.1 April 12, 2002

(Hardwick, Bolton 1997)   M. Hardwick, R. Bolton: The Industrial Virtual Enterprise, Communications of the ACM, September 1997

(Haren 2007)   V. Haren: TOGAF Version 8.1.1 Enterprise Edition — Study Guide, Van Haren Publishing, August 2007

(Heinisch, Simons 2004)   C. Heinisch, M. Simons: Telematics-moderated Software Download in Automotive Controllers, Steinbeis Transfer Center for Software Technology, 2004

(HL7V3 1998)   American National Standards Institute: HL7 Version 3 Statement of Principles, 1998

(Hohpe, Wolf 2004)   G. Hohpe, B. Woolf: Enterprise Integration Patterns, Addison-Wesley, 2004

(Inmon, Nesavich 2008)   W.H. Inmon, A. Nesavich: Tapping into Unstructured Data, Prentice Hall, 2008

(JCASpec 2003)   Connector Architecture Expert Group: J2EE Connector Architecture Specification, Version 1.5, Sun Microsystems, Inc., November 2003

(June 2005)   R. Jung: Architectures for Data Integration, German university-Publisher, 2005

(Liebhart et al. 2007)   D. Liebhart, G. Schmutz, M. Lattmann, M. Heinisch, M. Könings, M. Kölliker, P. Pakull, P. Welkenbach: Architecture Blueprints: A Guide for Construction of software systems with Java Spring, .NET, ADF, Forms, and SOA, Hanser, May 2007

(Lindsay 2008)   B.G. Lindsay: Jim Gray at IBM – The Transaction Processing Revolution, SIGMOD Record, June 2008, Vol. 37, No. 2

References

(Linthicum 1999) *D.S Linthicum.:* How to Select a Message Broker, e-biz Journal, 9.1.1999

(Linthicum 2000) *D.S Linthicum.:* Enterprise Application Integration, Addison-Wesley Professional, Dez. 2000

(Konsynski 1993) *B.R. Konsynski:* Strategic control in the extended enterprise, IBM Systems Journal VOL 32, NO 1, 1993

(Kirchhof et al. 2003) *A. Kirchhof, T. Gurzki, H. Hinderer, J, Vlachakis:* What is a Portal? — Definition and Use of Enterprise Portals, White Paper, Fraunhofer IAO, 2003

(Knappe et al. 2003) *M. Knappe, O. Koch, C Schneider:* Business Integration— Foundations of distributed IT Infrastructure, CTI Whitepaper, Januar 2003

(Krawczyk 2006) *M. Krawczyk:* Mastering IDoc Business Scenarios with SAP XI, SAP Press, October 2006

(Lam, Shankararaman 2007) *W. H. Lam, V. Shankararaman:* Enterprise Architecture and Integration: Methods, Implementation, and Technologies, IGI Global, May 2007

(Lee et al. 2003) *J. Lee, K. Siau, S. Hong:* Enterprise Integration with ERP and EAI, Communications of the ACM, February 2003, Vol.46, No.2

(Lublinsky 2002) *B. Lublinsky:* Approaches to B2B Integration, EAI Journal, 2002

(Luckham 2002) *D. Luckham:* The Power of Events: An Introduction to Complex Event Processing in Distributed Enterprise, Addison-Wesley Professional, May 2002

(Misek, Purdy 2006) *R. Misek, J. Purdy:* Coherence 3.3 User Guide, Oracle Corp. 2006

(Moser 2003) *G. Moser:* SAP R/3 Interfacing Using BAPIs; A Practical Guide to Working within the SAP Business Framework, GWV-Vieweg, October 2003

(Mühl et al. 2006) *G. Mühl, L. Fiege, P.R. Pietzuch:* Distributed Event-Based Systems, Springer 2006

[Nussdorfer, Martin 2003] *R: Nussdorfer, W. Martin:* RTE-Real-Time Oriented IT Architecture, EAI Forum, 2003

(Nussdorfer, Martin 2006) *R: Nussdorfer, W. Martin:* Role of Portals in a Service-Oriented Architecture, iBonD — intelligend Business on Demand — Series, March 2006

(OGSi 2003) *Open Service Gateway initiative:* OGSi Service Platfrom, Release 3 Specification, 2003

(OMG 2008) *Object Management Group:* Business Process Modeling Notation, V1.1, OMG 2008

(OpenGroup 1991) *The Open Group:* Distributed Transaction Processing: The XA Specification, X/Open Company Ltd. 1991

(Pape 2006) *Ch. Pape:* Enterprise Application Integration (EAI), University of Karlsruhe — Faculty of Computer Science and Business, 2006

(Patil, Newcorner 2003) *S. Patil, E. Newcorner*: ebXML and Web Services, IEEE Internet Computing, May-June 2003

(Puschmann 2004) *T. Puschmann:* Prozessportale — Architecture for networking with Customers and suppliers, Springer, Berlin, 2004

(Quema et al. 2003) *V. Quema, R. Balter, L. Lellissard, D. Feliot, A. Freyssinet, S. Lacourte:* Administration and Deployment Tools in a Message-Oriented Middleware, INRIA, France 2003

(Rahm 1994) *E. Rahm:* Multi-computer Database Systems: Fundamentals of Distributed and Parallel Database Processing, Addison-Wesley, 1994

(Ring, Ward-Dutton 1999) *K. Ring, N. Ward-Dutton:* Enterprise Application Integration: Making the Right Connections, Ovum Consulting Research 05/1999

(Rotem-Gal-Oz 2007) *A. Rotem-Gal-Oz:* SOA Patterns, Manning Publications 2007

(Russel et Al. 2006) *N. Russell, A. ter Hofstede, W. van der Aalst, and N. Mulyar:* Workflow Control-Flow Patterns: A Revised View. BPM Center Report BPM-06-22, BPMcenter.org, 2006

(Saad 2003) *A. Saad*: Protoyping in the BMW Car IT GmbH, JavaSpectrum, 2/2003

(Sailer 2001) *M. Sailer:* Requirements, Development, and Trends in Enterprise Application Integration (EAI), SerCon GmbH 2001

(Scheer et Al. 2006) *A.-W. Scheer, W. Jost, H. Hess, A. Kronz:* Corporate Performance Management, ARIS in Practice, Spinger 2006

(Scheer, Werth 2005) *Scheer, A.-W., Werth, D.:* Business Process Management and Business Rules, Institute of Information Management,, Saarbrucken, February 2005

(Ten-Hove, Walker 2005) *R. Ten-Hove, P. Walker:* Java Business Integration (JBI 1.0), Sun Microsystems Inc. 18 August, 2005

References

(Thomson 1997)   J. *Thomson.:* Avoiding the Middleware Muddle—Taking the guesswork out of tool selection, IEEE Software, November/December 1997

(Viehmann 2008)   H. *Viehmann:* From CQL to CEP to BAM — Oracle's Event Processing Platform now and in the (near) Future, Oracle Corp. 2008

(Wallrab 2005)   A. *Wallrab:* JSR-208: Java Business Integration, Sun Microsystems 2005

(Wakelin et al. 2002)   P. *Wakelin, M. Keen. R. Johnson, D.C. Diaz:* Java Connectors for CICS: Featuring the J2EE Architecture, IBM RedBook, March 2002

(White 2004)   S.A.: *White.:* Introduction to BPMN, BPTrends, July 2004

(Wütherich et al. 2008)   G. *Wütherich, N. Hartmann, B. Kolb, M. Lübken:* The OSGi Service Platform, dpunkt Publishing 2008

(Yuan et al. 2006)   J. *Yuan, A. Baharmi, C. Wang, M. Murray, A. Hunt:* A Semantic Information Integration Tool Suite, ACM VLDB 06 Conference Proceedings, 2006

(Zachmann 2007)   J. A. *Zachman:* The Framework For Enterprise Architecture: Background, Description and Utility, Zachmann International 2007

(Zeidler 2007)   A. *Zeidler:* Event-based Middleware for Pervasive Computing. Foundations, Concepts, Design, Vdm Publishing Dr. Müller, 2007

Index

Symbols

.NET 3.0
  about 188
  components 188-192
.NET 3.0, components
  Enterprise Single Sign On 191
  Entity Framework 191
  OData and WCF Data Services 192
  Trivadis TMDA 192
  Windows Communication Foundation 192
  Workflow Foundation (WF) 192

A

A2A 7, 9, 10
ABCS, AIA components 179
ABM, AIA components 179
Accelerating Advertising Processes in the Digital Age. *See* AdsML, transport formats
ACID 24, 65
Adapter Framework 189
adapters, Oracle Fusion Middleware components 94, 174
ADO.NET, transport protocols 117
AdsML, transport formats 118
agents
  about 54
  execution patterns 54
aggregator 148
AIA
  about 178
  components 179, 180
AIA, components
  Application Business Connector Service 179
  Composite Application Validation System 179
ANSI/ISO SQL standard
  levels 66
anycast, routing scheme 26
Apache Camel, Spring framework components 196
Apache Hadoop, Spring framework components 196
Apache ODE, Spring framework components 196
application and information view 95
Application Business Connector Service. *See* ABCS, AIA components
Application Business Message. *See* ABM, AIA components
application level
  process layer 127
application-to-application. *See* A2A
AQ 164
architecture blueprint 94
asynchronous receiver 124
atomicity 65
Atomicity, Consistency, Isolation, Durability. *See* ACID
Atomikos, Spring framework components 196
ATOM protocol 150
AtomPub 192
Atom Publishing Protocol. *See* AtomPub

B

B2B 7, 9, 10
B2B, Oracle Fusion Middleware
    components 174
B2C
    B2Cabout 7, 9, 10
BAM 58, 184
BAM, BizTalk Server components 190
BAM, Oracle Fusion Middleware
    components 175
BAPI, transport formats 117
base technologies, middleware
    component-oriented middleware 24
    data-oriented middleware 24
    message-oriented middleware 24
    remote procedure call 24
    transaction-oriented middleware 24
BEA 84
BEP 182
BizTalk Accelerators, BizTalk Server
    components 189
BizTalk Adapters, BizTalk Server
    components 189
BizTalk Server
    about 188
    components 188, 189
BizTalk Server, components
    BizTalk Accelerators 189
    BizTalk Adapters 189
    BizTalk Server Engine 189
    BRE 189
    Business Activity Monitoring 190
    Infopath 190
    Orchestration Designer for Business
        Analysts 190
    SharePoint Server 190
    SharePoint Services 190
    StreamInsight 191
BizTalk Server Engine, BizTalk Server
    components
    messaging components 189
BPD 88
BPEL
    about 55, 62, 89
    business protocols 89
    executable business protocols 89
BPEL integration process 145
BPEL, Oracle Fusion Middleware
    components 175
BPEL process 147
BPM 188
BPMN
    about 62, 88
    example 88
    graphical elements 88
BPM, Oracle Fusion Middleware
    components 175
BRE, BizTalk Server components 189
Broadcast, routing scheme 9, 25
broker 158
broker pattern, EAI
    advantages 34
    disadvantages 34
    logical components 33
    publish/subscribe message flow 33
    uses 34
broker pattern, EII. *See* broker pattern, EAI
building blocks
    about 103
    in collection layer, adapter 103
    in collection layer, mapper 103
    in distributer layer, adapter 103
    in distributer layer, mapper 103
    in mediation layer, message translator 103
    in mediation layer, router 103
building blocks, collection/distribution
        layer
    adapter 119
    connector 119
    DAO 120
    data mapper 120
    mappers 119
building blocks, mediation layer
    canonical data model 122, 123
    message channels 125
    message construction 124
    message routing 126
    message transformations 126
Business Activity Monitoring. *See* BAM,
        Oracle Fusion Middleware
        components
Business Application Programming
        Interface. *See* BAPI, transport formats

Business event 167
Business Event Processing. *See* BEP
Business Glossary 187
Business Process Diagrams. *See* BPD
Business Process Execution Language. *See* BPEL
Business Process Management. *See* BPM
Business Process Modeling Notation. *See* BPMN
Business Rules, Oracle Fusion Middleware components 175
business-to-business. *See* B2B
business-to-consumer. *See* B2C

C

canonical model, building blocks
  competing consumers 124
  event-driven consumer 124
  message dispatcher 124
  message endpoint 124
  polling consumer 124
  selective consumer 124
CardSpace 188
CAVS, AIA components 179
CDC 153, 181
CEP
  about 47, 48, 157
  funnel model 48
CEP funnel model 49
Change Data Capture. *See* CDC 187
channel adapter 125
claim check 127
Coherence 175
collection/distribution layer, integration domain level
  about 118
  base technology, JCA 119
  base technology, SOD 119
  building blocks 119
  responsibility 118
communication layer, transport level
  base technology 114
  building blocks 114
  implementing, requirements 114
  responsibility 113

transportation formats, using as building blocks 117, 118
transportation protocols, using as building blocks 115-117
communication methods, middleware
  conversational (Dialog-Oriented) 23
  message passing 23
  message queuing 23
  publish/subscribe 23
  request/reply 23
Competing consumers 124
Complex Event Processing. *See* CEP
CEP, Oracle Fusion Middleware components 176
Composite Application Validation System. *See* CAVS, AIA components
Connection Managers, SSIS components 193
consistency 65
Content-based router 145
content enricher 127
Continuous Query Language. *See* CQL
Control Flow Elements, SSIS components
  containers 194
  Precedence constraints 194
  tasks 194
CQL 176
cron 128
Cronacle 128

D

DAO 120
DAO, Spring framework components 199
Data Access Object. *See* DAO
Data Flow Elements, SSIS components
  destinations 194
  sources 194
  transformations 194
data grids, grid computing
  domain entity 52
  domain object 52
  in-memory 51
data integration, patterns
  about 37
  federation pattern 37

population pattern 38
synchronization pattern 40
data integration scenarios
  business patterns 148
  federation business pattern, implementing 148
  population business pattern, implementing 151
  synchronization business pattern, implementing 155, 156
data mapper 120
DataPower Appliance 183
DataStage 187
DataStage MVS Edition 187
Data Transfer Object. *See* **DTO**
Data Transformation Services. *See* **DTS**
DCOM, transport protocols 117
dead letter channel 125
direct connection business pattern, EAI/EII scenarios
  about 140
  alternative flows 141
  primary flow 140
  synchronous to asynchronous, bridging from 141, 142
  trigger 140
direct connection pattern, EAI
  about 32
  advantages 32
  disadvantages 32
  logical pattern 32
  uses 33
direct connection pattern, EII. *See* **direct connection pattern, EAI**
Distributed Component Object Model. *See* **DCOM, transport protocols**
Distributed Transaction 61
distribution topologies, grid computing
  partitioned caches 53
  replicated caches 52
  replicated caches, advantages 52
  replicated caches, disadvantages 53
domain-driven design
  about 93
  objectives 93
DTO 85

DTS 192
durability 65

E

EAI
  about 7, 9, 12, 14
  broker pattern 33
  defining 14
  direct connection pattern 32
  integration levels 16
  Middleware products 15
  router pattern 35
  SOA, differentiating between 12
EAI/EII scenarios
  broker business pattern, implementing 142
  business patterns 140
  direct connection business pattern, implementing 140
  router business pattern, implementing 143
EBF 179
EBM 179
EBO 178, 179
EBS 180
ebXML, transport formats 117
Eclipse 3.0 73
EDA
  about 45, 46
  event processing 47
  scenarios 157
EDA scenarios
  event processing business pattern, implementing 157, 158
EdiFact, transport formats 117
EII
  about 7
  aspects 45
  broker pattern 33
  direct connection pattern 32-35
  implementing, patterns 31
  router pattern 35
EIS 76
EJB 80
EJB session bean 145
Electronic Business using XML. *See* **ebXML, transport formats**

Enterprise Application Integration. *See* EAI
Enterprise Business Flow. *See* EBF
Enterprise Business Message. *See* EBM
Enterprise Business Objects. *See* EBO
Enterprise Business Service. *See* EBS
Enterprise Information Integration. *See* EII
Enterprise Information Systems. *See* EIS
Enterprise JavaBean. *See* EJB
Enterprise Service Bus. *See* ESB
Enterprise Single Sign On, .NET 3.0 components 191
Entity Framework, .NET 3.0 components 191
EPC
  about 62, 87
  example 87
EPL 197
ESB
  about 9, 21, 176
  basic structure 22
  core functions 21
  product, functions 22
ESP 48
Esper, Spring framework components 197
ETL 38, 180
Event-driven architecture. *See* EDA
event-driven consumer 124
Event-Driven Process Chain. *See* EPC
event processing business pattern, EDA scenarios
  implementing, CEP used 157, 158
  variant with, two levels of CEP 158, 159
event processing, EDA
  about 47
  CEP 47, 48
  ESP 47, 48
  SEP 47, 48
Event Processing Language. *See* EPL
event processing pattern
  aggregation over windows 132
  Correlation (joins) 132
  database lookups 132
  database writes 132
  dynamic queries 133
  Event pattern matching 132
  filtering 131

hierarchical events 133
In-memory caching 131
state machines 133
Event Stream Processing. *See* ESP
execution patterns, agents
  data-grid aggregation 55
  data-grid-wide execution 55
  node-based execution 55
  parallel execution 55
  query-based execution 55
  targeted execution 54
Extended Enterprise 10
Extensible Stylesheet Language. *See* XSL
Extract, Transform, and Load. *See* ETL
Extreme Transaction Processing. *See* XTP

F

Failover 16
federation business pattern, data integration scenarios
  about 148, 149
  implementing, mashup process used 150
  mashup technology, using 149
  SOA-based implementation diagram 148, 149
federation pattern, data integration
  about 37
  calling applications 37
  diagrammatic representation 37
  federation building block 38
  source application 38
  uses 38
Federation Server 187
File Transfer Protocol. *See* FTP
FTP 164

G

GFS 196
Google File System. *See* GFS
graphical elements, BPMN
  artifacts 88
  connecting objects 88
  flow objects 88
  swimlanes 88
grid, defining 49

[211]

grid computing
  about 49
  basic model 50
  data grids 51
  distribution topologies 52
  features 50
  tasks, distributed caching 50
  tasks, event-driven processing 50
  tasks, processing 50
  uses 55
grid computing business pattern
  combining with direct connection pattern and ESB 160
  implementing 160
grid computing scenarios
  about 159
  business pattern, implementing 160
grid computing, uses
  complex real-time intelligence 57
  data access buffers 56
  data access virtualization 56
  data format virtualization 56
  distributed master data management 56
  distributed transactional data cache (domain entities) 55
  distributed transactional object cache (domain entities) 55
  ESB notification service 56
  high performance backup and recovery 56
  maintenance window virtualization 56
  SOA grid 55
  storage access virtualization 56

H

Hibernate, Spring framework components 197
HL7, transport formats 117
hub-and-spoke architecture, integration architecture variants
  about 28, 29
  advantages 29
  disadvantages 29
  opportunities 29
  threats 29
Human Workflow, Oracle Fusion Middleware components 176

I

IaaS 57
IBM 84
IBM Information Management software
  about 186
  components 186-188
IBM Information Management software, components
  Business Glossary 187
  Change Data Capture 187
  Change Data Capture for Oracle Replication 187
  DataStage 187
  DataStage MVS Edition 187
  Federation Server 187
  Information Analyzer 187
  Information Service Director 187
  Metadata Server 187
  QualityStage 188
IBM Tivioli Workload Scheduler 128
IBM WebSphere
  about 182
  components 182-186
IBM WebSphere, components
  BEP 182
  CEP Detector Nodes 185
  DataPower Appliance 183
  InfoSphere MashupHub 183
  InfoSphere Streams 183
  solidDB 184
  Tivoli Netcool 184
  WebSphere Adapters 184
  WebSphere Business Monitor 184
  WebSphere Enterprise Service Bus 184
  WebSphere eXtreme Scale 184
  WebSphere Message Broker 185
  WebSphere Partner Gateway 185
  WebSphere Portal 185
  WebSphere Process Server 185
  WebSphere Service Registry and Repository 186
  WebSphere Transformation Extender 186
IDoc, transport formats 118
Infopath, BizTalk Server components 190
Information Analyzer 187

Information-as-a-Service. *See* IaaS
information flow 101
information flow, Trivadis Integration Architecture Blueprint
 different target system, routing to in communication layer 110
 different target system, routing to in mediation layer 109
 target, as source 108, 109
 task, sharing in mediation layer 110
 workflow building block, using 111
Information Service Director 187
InfoSphere MashupHub 183
InfoSphere Streams 183
integration
 A2A 7
 n about 7
 B2B 7
 B2C 7
 design patterns 8
 EAI 8
 ESB 8
 hub-and-spoke architecture 8
 pipeline architecture 8
 point-to-point architecture 8
 semantic integration 9
 types 9, 11
 XTP 8
integration architecture variants
 shub-and-spoke architecture 26
 pipeline architecture 27
 spoint-to-point architecture 26
 service-oriented architecture 27
integration domain
 business domains 93
 technical domains 93
integration domain level
 collection/distribution layer 118
 mediation layer 120
integration domain level, application and information view
 about 96
 mediation layer 96
Integration instead of isolation 2
integration levels, EAI
 integration on data level 16
 integration on object level 16

integration on process level 16
integration solution, modernizing
 about 163
 confirmation, receiving 165
 existing solution, evaluating 165
 initial situation 163-166
 new orders, sending 164
 new solution, evaluating 169
 SOA-based integration architecture 166-168
integration, types
 information portals 11
 shared business functions 12
 shared data 11
integration view
 connecting layer 100
 forwarding layer 100
 tasks 100
 transportation layer 100
invalid message channel 125
invoke command 168
isolation 65
isolation levels
 about 66
 read committed 67
 read uncommitted 68
 repeatable read 67
 serializable 66

J

Java Business Integration. *See* JBI
Java Connector Architecture. *See* JCA
Java Database Connectivity. *See* JDBC
Java Messaging Service. *See* JMS
Java Process Definition Language. *See* jPDL
Java Virtual Machine. *See* JVM
JBI
 about 62, 79
 components 80
 message exchange pattern, one-way 79
 message exchange pattern, reliable one-way 79
 message exchange pattern, request/optional response 79
 message exchange pattern, request/response 79
 tasks 79

JBI, components
 binding components 80
 delivery channel 81
 JBI container 80
 JBI environment 80
 NMR 80
 normalized message 81
 pluggable components 80
 service engine 80
JBoss Rules, Spring framework components 197
JCA
 about 62, 76, 174
 components 77
 contracts 78
 uses 76
JCA, components
 Common Client Interface (CCI) 77
 Container-Component Contracts 77
 Enterprise Information System 77
 resource adapter 77
 System-Level Contracts 77
JCA, contracts
 connection management 78
 life cycle management 78
 message inflow management 79
 security management 78
 transaction inflow management 78
 transaction management 78
 work management 78
JDBC 170
JMS 48, 81, 145
JMS adapter 145
jPDL 197
JSR 235 84
JVM 181

K

Key Performance Indicators. *See* **KPIs**
KM
 Check KM 181
 Integration KM 181
 Journalizing KM 181
 Loading KM 181
 Reverse Engineering KM 181
 Service KM 181
Knowledge modules. *See* **KM**
KPIs 184

L

L7 OSB 177
Layer 7 Oracle Service Bus. *See* **L7 OSB**
layered architecture
 building block 92
 layer 92
layers, allocating to levels
 application level 112
 communication layer 111
 integration domain level 112
 media and collection/distribution layers 111
 process layers 112
 transportation layer 112

M

mapper 94
mediation layer, integration domain level
 base technologies 121
 building blocks 121
 implementing, requirements 121
 responsibility 120
Mediator
 benefits 101
 pattern, defining 101
Mediator, Oracle Fusion Middleware components 176
message broker
 about 18,
 availability attribute 19
 failure handling attributes 19
 hub-and-spoke architecture 19
 logical ports 18
 message routing 19
 message transformation 19
 modifiability attribute 19
 performance attribute 19
 scalability attribute 19
message channels, building blocks
 channel adapter 125
 dead letter channel 125
 invalid message channel 125

point-to-point channel 125
publish/subscribe channel 125
message context data 81
message dispatcher pattern 124, 142
message endpoint 124
Message flows 156
Message-Oriented Middleware. See MOM
message router 158
message router, building blocks
    aggregator 126
    content-based router 126
    dynamic router 126
    message filter 126
    pipes-and-filters 126
    recipient list 126
    resequence 126
    splitter 126
message transformation, building blocks
    claim check 127
    content enricher 127
    correlation identifier 125
    message translator 127
    Request/reply 124
    return address 125
message translator 127
messaging, attributes
    availability 16
    failure handling 16
    modifiability 17
    performance 17
    scalability 17
messaging infrastructure
    components, customer 20
    components, event management 20
    components, intermediate queue 20
    components, local queue 20
    components, message management 20
    components, producer 20
    diagrammatic representation 20
Metadata Server 187
Microsoft 89
Microsoft BizTalk. See BizTalk Server
Microsoft Message Queues. See MSMQ
Microsoft .NET Architecture Blueprint 171
Microsoft Office SharePoint Server. See MOSS

Microsoft SQL Server Integration Services. See SSIS
middleware
    about 9, 23
    base technologies 24
    communication methods 23
    database gateways 24
    database replication 24
    direct messaging 24
    message infrastructure 24
    message queue systems 24
    object request brokers 24
    peer-to-peer, API 24
    remote procedure calls 24
    routing schemes 25
MOM 141
MOSS 190
MSMQ 192
Mule, Spring framework components 197
multicast, routing scheme 18, 26

N

Nagios, Spring framework components 197
Near real-time 23
Next Generation SOA 46
NMR 80
Normalized Message Router. See NMR
notation
    capacity planning extensions 137, 138
    configuration parameters 136
    granularity levels, visualizing 135
    scenarios, representing 134
    transaction boundaries, representing 136
    valid notations, diagram 134

O

OData and WCF Data Services, .NET 3.0 components 192
ODI
    about 180
    components 180, 181
    ETL architecture 180
ODI, components
    knowledge 181
    knowledge modules 181

[215]

repository 181
Scheduler Agent 181
OGSi 62
OLAP 46
OLTP 46
Online Analytical Processing. *See* OLAP
Online Transaction Processing. *See* OLTP
Open Grid Services infrastructure. *See* OGSi
Open Service Gateway initiative. *See* OSGi
Open Service-Oriented Architecture. *See* OSOA
Open Source Job Scheduler 128
Oracle 89
Oracle ADF Architecture Blueprint 171
Oracle Advanced Queuing. *See* AQ
Oracle Application Integration Architecture. *See* AIA
Oracle Data Integrator. *See* ODI
Oracle Fusion Middleware
  about 173
  components 174-178
  components, diagrammatic representation 174
  Oracle Application Integration Architecture 178
Oracle Fusion Middleware, components
  adapters 174
  B2B 174
  BAM 175
  BPEL 175
  BPM 175
  Business Rules 175
  Coherence 175
  Complex Event Processing 176
  Human Workflow 176
  Mediator 176
  OSB 176
  SCA 177
  SDO 177
  TimesTen 177
  TopLink 177
  User Messaging Service 178
  WebCenter 178
Oracle Service Bus. *See* OSB
Oracle Service Bus Appliance. *See* OSBA
Oracle Service Bus Appliance, Oracle
  Fusion Middleware components 177
orchestrating 106
Orchestration Designer for Business Analysts, BizTalk Server components 190
OSB 176
OSBA 177
OSGi
  about 72
  architecture 74
  architecture, layers 72
  bundles 75
  bundles, collaborating 76
  collaborative model 76
  collaborative software environment 72
  component model 72
  features 72
  framework 73
  service platform 73
  specifications 73
OSGi, architecture
  execution environment 74
  life cycle management 74
  modules 74
  service registry 75
OSGi, Spring framework components 198
OSOA 84

P

partitioned caches
  load-balanced 54
  location transparency 54
  partitioned 53
patterns, SDO
  Data Access Object (DAO) 86
  Data Transfer Object (DTO) 86
  disconnected data usage 86
  Entity object (EO) 86
  optimistic concurrency semantics data access 86
PIP 180
pipeline architecture, integration architecture variants
  about 29
  advantages 30
  disadvantages 30

opportunities 30
themes 30
point-to-point architecture, integration architecture variants
  about 27
  advantages 28
  disadvantages 28
  opportunities 28
  threats 28
point-to-point channel 125
polling consumer 124
population business pattern, data integration scenarios
  about 151
  CDC method, using 153, 154
  encapsulating, as web service 152
  SOA-based population pattern variant, triggered by CDC 154, 155
population pattern, data integration
  about 38
  diagrammatic representation 39
  population component 39
  source applications 39
  target application 39
  uses 39
process integration business pattern, service-oriented integration
  batch-driven integration process, variant with 146
  externalized business rules, variant with 146
Process Integration Pack. *See* **PIP**
process integration pattern, service-oriented integration
  about 42
  advantages 43
  disadvantages 43
  source applications, components 42
  target applications, components 43
  uses 43
  variants, external business rules 44
  variants, parallel process pattern 43
process layer, application level
  base technologies 128
  building blocks 128
  implementing, requirements 127
  responsibility 127

process layer, building blocks
  event processing pattern 131
  job scheduler 128
  portal 128
  workflow 129
process layer, Trivadis Integration Architecture Blueprint
  about 106, 107
  adding 105
  building blocks 107, 108
  orchestrating 106
process modeling
  about 86
  applications 90
  BPEL 89
  BPMN 88
  EPC 87
publisher
  about 17
  availability attribute 18
  failure handling attribute 18
  modifiability attribute 18
  performance attribute 18
  scalability attribute 18
publish/subscribe channel 125
publish/subscribe pattern 142

Q

QoS 97
Quality of Service. *See* **QoS**
QualityStage 188
Quartz 128
Quartz Scheduler, Spring framework components 198
queuing mechanism 163
Query language 157

R

Radio Frequency Identification. *See* **RFID**
real-time enterprise. *See* **RTE**
Reliable messaging 18
Remote Function Call. *See* **RFC**
replication pattern. *See* **synchronization pattern, data integration**
repository, ODI components 181

[217]

resequence 126
RFC 162
RFID 47
roles
   collection layer 102
   communication layer 102
   distribution layer 102
   mediation layer 102
RosettaNet, transport formats 118
router pattern, EAI
   about 35
   advantages 36
   disadvantages 36
   logical components 35
   uses 36
router pattern, EII. *See* router pattern, EAI
routing schemes, middleware
   about 9
   anycast 26
   broadcast 25
   multicast 26
   unicast 25
RSS feed 150
RTE 45

S

SAP 89
SAP Exchange Infrastructure. *See* SAP XI
SAP system
   connecting to 161, 162
SAP XI 162
SCA
   about 62, 81, 177
   composites 84
   elements 83
   specifications 82
SCA, elements
   binding 83
   implementation 83
   property 83
   reference 83
   service 83
   wire 83
SCA specifications
   assembly model 82
   binding specification 82
   client and implementation 82
   diagram 82
   policy framework 82
SCDL 84
SCXML 196
SDO
   about 62, 84, 177
   architecture 85
   patterns 86
SDO, architecture
   data access service 85
   data graph 85
   data object 85
   diagram 85
selective consumers 124
semantic integration
   about 13
   model-based semantic repositories 14
   problems 13
SEP 48
Separation of Concerns. *See* SOC; *See* SoC
Service Component Architecture. *See* SCA
Service Component Definition Language.
      See SCDL
Service Data Objects. *See* SDO
Service Level Agreements. *See* SLA
service-oriented architecture, integration
      architecture variants
   about 30
   advantages 31
   disadvantages 31
   opportunities 31
   threats 31
service-oriented integration
   business patterns 144
   pattern 42
   process integration business pattern,
      implementing 144, 145
   process integration pattern 42
   workflow integration pattern 42, 44
servlet 84
shared business functions
   EAI 12
   SOA 12
shared data
   data transfer 11
   file replication 11

shared database 11
shared data storage 52
SharePoint Services, BizTalk Server
    components 190
Siebel 89
Simple Event Processing. See SEP
Skiddle 84
SLA 50
SOA 12, 15
  EAI, differentiating between 12
SoC 33, 100
solidDB 184
Solid State Disk. See SSD
splitter 148
Spring Architecture Blueprint 171
Spring Batch, Spring framework
    components 198
Spring framework
  about 195
  components 196-199
Spring framework, components
  Apache Camel 196
  Apache Commons SCXML 196
  Apache Hadoop 196
  Apache ODE 196
  Atomikos 196
  DAO 199
  Esper 197
  Hibernate 197
  JBoss Rules 197
  jBPM 197
  Mule 197
  Nagios 197
  OSGi 198
  OS Workflow 198
  Quartz Scheduler 198
  Spring Batch 198
  Spring Integration 198
  Spring ORM 199
  Spring Security 199
  SpringSource Application Platform 199
  WSO2 Business Activity Monitor 199
  WSO2 Data Services Server 199
  WSO2 Governance Registry 200
Spring Integration, Spring framework
    components 198

Spring ORM, Spring framework
    components 199
Spring Security, Spring framework
    components 199
SpringSource Application Platform, Spring
    framework components 199
Spring Webservice Framework 170
SSD
  about 59
  benefits 59
  uses 59
SSIS
  about 192
  components 193, 194
SSIS, components
  Connection Managers 193
  Control Flow Elements 194
  Data Flow Elements 194
State Chart XML. See SCXML
StreamInsight, BizTalk Server components
    191
subscriber 17
SWIFT, transport formats 117
synchronization pattern, data integration
  about 40
  diagrammatic representation 40
  multi-step synchronization 41
  source applications 41
  target application 40
  uses 41
synchronous receiver 124

T

Tangosol Coherence. See Coherence
technical integration domain 92
TimesTen, Oracle Fusion Middleware
    components 177
Tivoli Netcool 184
TMDA 192
TopLink, Oracle Fusion Middleware
    components 177
transactional systems
  about 63
  atomic transactions 65
  commit 64
  completing 64

example 63
rollback 64
transaction coordinator 65
transaction manager 65
transactions
about 63
isolation levels 63, 66
phantom read 68
transactional systems 63
two-phase commit 63, 69
XA transaction 63, 70
transport formats
AdsML 118
BAPI 117
ebXML 117
EdiFact 117
HL7 117
IDoc 118
RosettaNet 118
SWIFT 117
transport level, Trivadis Architecture Blueprints
about 96
application llevel 96
assembly 97
BAM 97
communication level 96
deployment 97
governance 97
integration domain level 96
management 97
QoS 97
security 97
transaction 97
transport protocols
ADO.NET 117
DCOM 117
FTP 115
HTTP 115
IMAP 116
IOP 115
iSCSI 116
JDBC 115
JMS 115
MSMQ 116
Net8 116
NFS 116

ODBC 115
POP3 116
RMI 115
SMB 116
SMTP 116
soap 116
SQL*NET 116
115
UCP 115
XML-RPC 116
XMPP 116
Trivadis Architecture Blueprints
about 169
applications 95
non-transactional information storage 95
Spring framework based example 170
transactional information storage 95
transport level 96
Trivadis Integration Architecture Blueprint
about 91
adapter 94
application and information view 95
application and integration view, differentiating between 99
application and integration view, tasks 100
architecture blueprint 94
blueprints, structuring 94
building blocks 92, 103
collection and distribution layer, combining 104
components 91
direction changing, in information flow 104, 105
domain-driven design 93
information flow 101, 108
integration blueprint, layers 98
integration blueprint, levels 98
integration blueprint, tasks 97
integration domain 93
layered architecture 92
layers, allocating to levels 111
mapper 94
overview diagram 95
process layer, adding 105, 106
roles 101
standards 92
technical integration domain 92

Trivadis Managed Data Access. *See* TMDA
Trivadis TMDA, .NET 3.0 components 192
two-phase commit
  about 69, 70
  commit phase 69
  commit request 69
  protocol 70
TX 186

U

unicast, routing scheme 25
UPDATE command 165
User Messaging Service, Oracle Fusion Middleware components 178

V

Virtual Enterprise 10
visualization. *See* notation

W

WCF 188
WebCenter, Oracle Fusion Middleware components 178
Web Service Definition Language. *See* WSDL
Web Services Enhancements. *See* WSE
WebSphere Adapters 184
WebSphere Enterprise Service Bus 184
WebSphere eXtreme Scale 184
WebSphere Message Broker 185
WebSphere Partner Gateway 185
WebSphere Portal 185
WebSphere Process Server 185
WebSphere Service Registry and Repository 186
WebSphere Transformation Extender. *See* TX
WF 188
Windows Communication Foundation. *See* WCF
Windows SharePoint Services. *See* WSS
Windows Workflow Foundation. *See* WF
workflow, building blocks
  advanced branching patterns 129, 130
  basic control patterns 129
  cancellation patterns 131
  Multiple instances (MI) patterns 130
  state-based patterns 130
  structural patterns 130
  synchronization patterns 129, 130
Workflow Foundation, .NET 3.0 components 192
workflow integration pattern, service-oriented integration
  diagrammatic representation 44
  variants, parallel workflow 44
WSDL 83
WSE 192
WSFL 89
WSO2 Business Activity Monitor, Spring Framework components 199
WSO2 Data Services Server, Spring Framework components 199
WSO2 Governance Registry, Spring Framework components 200
WSS 190

X

XA35 device 183
XA transaction
  about 70
  atomic transaction, comparing with 71
  Die X/Open XA specification 70
  using 71
XI50 device 183
XLANG 89
XLS 80
XS40 device 183
XTP
  about 7, 49, 57
  and CEP 58
  applications 58
  growth areas 58
  SOA grid 58

Z

zero latency access 52

Thank you for buying
Service-Oriented Architecture: An Integration Blueprint

About Packt Publishing

Packt, pronounced 'packed', published its first book "Mastering phpMyAdmin for Effective MySQL Management" in April 2004 and subsequently continued to specialize in publishing highly focused books on specific technologies and solutions.

Our books and publications share the experiences of your fellow IT professionals in adapting and customizing today's systems, applications, and frameworks. Our solution based books give you the knowledge and power to customize the software and technologies you're using to get the job done. Packt books are more specific and less general than the IT books you have seen in the past. Our unique business model allows us to bring you more focused information, giving you more of what you need to know, and less of what you don't.

Packt is a modern, yet unique publishing company, which focuses on producing quality, cutting-edge books for communities of developers, administrators, and newbies alike. For more information, please visit our website: www.packtpub.com.

About Packt Enterprise

In 2010, Packt launched two new brands, Packt Enterprise and Packt Open Source, in order to continue its focus on specialization. This book is part of the Packt Enterprise brand, home to books published on enterprise software – software created by major vendors, including (but not limited to) IBM, Microsoft and Oracle, often for use in other corporations. Its titles will offer information relevant to a range of users of this software, including administrators, developers, architects, and end users.

Writing for Packt

We welcome all inquiries from people who are interested in authoring. Book proposals should be sent to author@packtpub.com. If your book idea is still at an early stage and you would like to discuss it first before writing a formal book proposal, contact us; one of our commissioning editors will get in touch with you.

We're not just looking for published authors; if you have strong technical skills but no writing experience, our experienced editors can help you develop a writing career, or simply get some additional reward for your expertise.

SOA Patterns with BizTalk Server 2009

ISBN: 978-1-847195-00-5   Paperback: 400 pages

Implement SOA strategies for BizTalk Server solutions

1. Discusses core principles of SOA and shows them applied to BizTalk solutions
2. The most thorough examination of BizTalk and WCF integration in any available book
3. Leading insight into the new WCF SQL Server Adapter, UDDI Services version 3, and ESB Guidance 2.0

SOA Governance

ISBN: 978-1-847195-86-9   Paperback: 228 pages

The key to successful SOA adoption in your organization

1. Learn about SOA Governance to achieve SOA success in your company
2. Follow a fictitious company's journey of SOA Governance adoption
3. Learn to choose the right people, processes, and policies to achieve successful SOA Governance within your company
4. Understand the services and strategies used to achieve consistent results

Please check www.PacktPub.com for information on our titles

WCF Multi-tier Services Development with LINQ

ISBN: 978-1-847196-62-0 Paperback: 384 pages

Build SOA applications on the Microsoft platform in this hands-on guide

1. Master WCF and LINQ concepts by completing practical examples and apply them to your real-world assignments
2. First book to combine WCF and LINQ in a multi-tier real-world WCF service
3. Ideal for beginners who want to build scalable, powerful, easy-to-maintain WCF services

Business Process Driven SOA using BPMN and BPEL

ISBN: 978-1-847191-46-5 Paperback: 328 pages

From Business Process Modeling to Orchestration and Service Oriented Architecture

1. Understand business process management and how it relates to SOA
2. Understand advanced business process modeling and management with BPMN and BPEL
3. Work with tools that support BPMN and BPEL (Oracle BPA Suite)
4. Transform BPMN to BPEL and execute business processes on the SOA platform

Please check www.PacktPub.com for information on our titles

Lightning Source UK Ltd.
Milton Keynes UK
UKOW03f1837130115

244442UK00009B/331/P